"Why would an account of the daily life of monks and their dynamic, inspiring, also controversial, Abbot capture the religious imagination and become one of the most popular books of seventeenth-century France? Thanks to David Bell's excellent translation and notes we are now able to find out for ourselves. This riveting account of a fascinating world unknown to most of us will delight monastic scholars, historians, and anyone interested in the origins of Trappist life and thought. It is an engaging piece of work, which reads like a historical novel. Indeed, Bell has given us a treasure in bringing this work into English."

— Abbess Kathy DeVico
Our Lady of the Redwoods Abbey
Whitethorn, California

CISTERCIAN STUDIES SERIES: NUMBER TWO HUNDRED SEVENTY-FOUR

Everyday Life at La Trappe under Armand-Jean de Rancé

A Translation,
with Introduction and Notes,
of
André Félibien des Avaux's
Description De L'abbaye De La Trappe (1689)

David N. Bell

Cistercian Publications
www.cistercianpublications.org

LITURGICAL PRESS
Collegeville, Minnesota
www.litpress.org

A Cistercian Publications title published by Liturgical Press

Cistercian Publications
Editorial Offices
161 Grosvenor Street
Athens, Ohio 45701
www.cistercianpublications.org

Scripture texts in this work are translated by David N. Bell.

© 2018 by Order of Saint Benedict, Collegeville, Minnesota. All rights reserved. No part of this book may be reproduced in any form, by print, microfilm, microfiche, mechanical recording, photocopying, translation, or any other means, known or yet unknown, for any purpose except brief quotations in reviews, without the previous written permission of Liturgical Press, Saint John's Abbey, PO Box 7500, Collegeville, Minnesota 56321-7500. Printed in the United States of America.

Library of Congress Cataloging-in-Publication Data

Names: Felibien, Andre, sieur des Avaux et de Javercy, 1619–1695, author. | Bell, David N., 1943– translator.
Title: Everyday life at La Trappe under Armand-Jean de Rance : a translation, with introduction and notes of Andre Felibien des Avaux's Description de L'Abbaye de La Trappe (1689) / David N. Bell.
Other titles: Description de L'Abbaye de La Trappe. English
Description: Collegeville, Minnesota : Cistercian Publications, 2018. | Series: Cistercian studies series ; Number two hundred seventy-four | Includes bibliographical references and index.
Identifiers: LCCN 2018004625 (print) | LCCN 2018040969 (ebook) | ISBN 9780879071745 (ebook) | ISBN 9780879072742
Subjects: LCSH: Abbaye de la Trappe (Soligny-la-Trappe, France). | Trappists—France. | Monastic and religious life—France—History—17th century—Sources. | Rance, Armand Jean Le Bouthillier de, 1626–1700.
Classification: LCC BX2615.A2355 (ebook) | LCC BX2615.A2355 F4513 2018 (print) | DDC 271/.12504423—dc23
LC record available at https://lccn.loc.gov/2018004625

Contents

List of Abbreviations   vii

Introduction   1
    Figure 1: Plan of the Abbey of La Trappe, with east
        at the top   26
    Figure 2: The Interior of the Church of La Trappe   27

Description of the Abbey of La Trappe
    The Bookseller to the Reader   43
    Description of the Abbey of La Trappe (1689)   45

Appendix:
    Discourse on the Reform of the Abbey of La Trappe   155

Select Bibliography   161

Index of Subjects   163

Index of Names and Places   166

Index of Scriptural Citations   174

List of Abbreviations

Bell, *Library* = David N. Bell. *The Library of the Abbey of La Trappe from the Twelfth Century to the French Revolution, with an Annotated Edition of the 1752 Catalogue.* Turnhout: Brepols; Cîteaux – Commentarii cistercienses, 2014.

Bell, *Rancé* = David N. Bell. *Understanding Rancé: The Spirituality of the Abbot of La Trappe in Context.* Cistercian Studies Series, 205. Kalamazoo, MI: Cistercian Publications, 2005.

Charencey = Charles-Félix-Hyacinthe, comte de Charencey. *Histoire de l'abbaye de la Grande-Trappe.* Documents sur la Province du Perche; ii, 6. Mortagne: Georges Meaux, 1896–1911.

Choisselet/Vernet = Danièle Choisselet and Placide Vernet, eds./trans. *Les Ecclesiastica Officia cisterciens du XIIème siècle.* La Documentation cistercienne, 22. Reiningue: Abbaye d'Œlenberg, 1989.

Constitutions = *Constitutions de l'abbaye de La Trappe.* Paris: Michel Le Petit & Estienne Michallet, 1671.

CS = Cistercian Studies series. Cistercian Publications.

CSQ = *Cistercian Studies Quarterly*

Denzinger = Heinrich Denzinger. *Enchiridion symbolorum definitionum et declarationum de rebus fidei et morum. Compendium of Creeds, Definitions and Declarations on Matters of Faith and Morals. Latin – English.* 43rd ed. Ed. Peter Hünermann. San Francisco: Ignatius Press, 2012.

DLF XVII = *Dictionnaire des lettres françaises. Le XVIIe siècle*. Ed. Patrick Dandrey. Paris: Fayard, 1951; repr. with revisions 1996.

Dubois, *Histoire* = Louis Dubois. *Histoire civile, religieuse et littéraire de l'abbaye de La Trappe, et des autres Monastères de la même Observance qui se sont établis tant en France que dans les pays étrangers avant et depuis la révolution de 1789, et notamment de l'Abbaye de Mellerai; suivie de chartes et d'autres pièces justificatives, la plupart inédites*. Paris: Raynal, 1824.

Dubois, *Rancé* = Louis Dubois. *Histoire de l'abbé de Rancé et de sa réforme*. 2nd ed. Paris: Poussielgue Frères, 1869.

Gervaise, *Jugement critique* = Armand-François Gervaise. *Jugement critique, mais équitable des vies de feu M. l'abbé de Rancé, réformateur de l'abbaye de La Trappe. Écrites par les Sieurs Marsollier et Maupeou. Divisé en deux parties où l'on voit toutes les fautes qu'ils ont commises contre la vérité de l'Histoire, contre le bon sens, contre la vray-semblance [sic], contre l'honneur même de M. de Rancé, et de la Maison de La Trappe*. London [= Troyes or Reims]: [n.d.], 1742.

Krailsheimer, *Legacy* = Alban J. Krailsheimer. *Rancé and the Trappist Legacy*. CS 86. Kalamazoo, MI: Cistercian Publications, 1985.

Krailsheimer, *Rancé* = Alban J. Krailsheimer. *Armand-Jean de Rancé, Abbot of La Trappe. His Influence in the Cloister and the World*. Oxford: Clarendon Press, 1974.

L'Abbaye de La Trappe = Marie-Gérard Dubois, Alban J. Krailsheimer, Augustin-Hervé Laffay, Hugues de Seréville, and Philippe Siguret. *L'Abbaye Notre-Dame de La Trappe*. Meaucé: Amis du Perche, 2001.

Lekai, *Cistercians* = Louis J. Lekai, *The Cistercians. Ideals and Reality*. Kent, OH: Kent State University Press, 1977.

Lekai, *Rise* = Louis J. Lekai. *The Rise of the Cistercian Strict Observance in Seventeenth Century France*. Washington, DC: Catholic University of America Press, 1968.

PL = Patrologia Latina. Ed. J.-P. Migne. Paris.

Rancé, *Correspondance* = Abbé de Rancé. *Correspondance*. Ed. Alban J. Krailsheimer. 4 vols. Paris: Les Éditions du Cerf / Cîteaux – Commentarii cistercienses, 1993.The letters are cited by year, month, and day: e.g., Letter 910104 = 1691 January 4.

Règlemens = *Règlemens de l'abbaye de Nôtre-Dame de La Trappe en forme de Constitutions, avec des Réflexions, Et la Carte de Visite faite à N. D. des Clairets, par le R. P. Abbé de la Trappe*. Paris: Florentin Delaulne, 1718.

SBOp = Sancti Bernardi Opera. Ed. Jean Leclercq and H. M. Rochais. Rome: Editiones Cistercienses, 1968.

Tournoüer = Henri Tournoüer. *Bibliographie et iconographie de la Maison-Dieu Notre-Dame de La Trappe au diocèse de Sées, de Dom A.-J. Le Bouthillier de Rancé, Abbé et Réformateur de cette abbaye, et en général de tous les religieux du même monastère.* Documents sur la province du Perche, iv, 2. Mortagne: Marchand & Gilles/Georges Meaux, 1894–1896.

Waddell, *Texts* = Chrysogonus Waddell. *Narrative and Legislative Texts from Early Cîteaux. Latin Text in Dual Edition with English Translation and Notes*. Studia et Documenta, IX. Brecht: Cîteaux – Commentarii cistercienses, 1999.

Introduction

The *Description de l'abbaye de La Trappe*, first published at Paris in 1671, was one of the best-sellers of seventeenth-century France, and it remains the classic account of La Trappe under its most famous abbot. There were numerous editions, printings, and re-printings,[1] of which the two most important were the first, which appeared in 1671, and the "New Edition, with Figures," which appeared eighteen years later in 1689. The 1671 edition was published at Paris by Frédéric Léonard; the new edition by Jacques Le Febvre, also at Paris. The author (as we shall see) knew both La Trappe and its abbot well, and when the book first appeared Rancé was forty-five and had been a regular abbot of La Trappe for seven years. He was still abbot in 1689, though by this time his severe austerities had begun to take their toll, and ill health forced him to resign the abbacy in May 1695. He died five years and a few months later on October 27, 1700. The author of the *Description* had died on June 11, 1695, just a few weeks after Rancé had resigned as abbot. Who was this author?

The Author

Almost all the editions of the *Description* were published anonymously, but the overwhelming consensus is that it was

---

[1] See David N. Bell, *Understanding Rancé: The Spirituality of the Abbot of La Trappe in Context*, CS 205 (Kalamazoo, MI: Cistercian Publications, 2005), 312–13.

written by André Félibien, sieur des Avaux et de Javercy, one of the most distinguished art and architectural historians of the age of Louis XIV. There is, however, a problem. The 1683 edition was published at Lyon by Laurent Aubin and bears the title *Description de l'Abbaye de La Trappe avec Constitutions, les Réflexions sur icelles; la Mort de quelques Religieux de ce Monastère, Plusieurs Lettres du R. P. Abbé [de Rancé]; et une Brièfve Relation de l'Abbaye de Septfons*. In this volume, the *Description* is attributed to "le R[évérend]. P[ère]. Desmares Prestre de l'Oratoire."[2] Who was the Reverend Father Desmares, and how did his name come to appear as the author of the *Description*?

He was Toussaint-Guy-Joseph Desmares, born towards the end of 1599 at Vire in Lower Normandy.[3] He first studied at Caen and then, at an early age, entered the Oratory, where he placed himself under the direction of Pierre de Bérulle, then superior general of the congregation and later cardinal. He made an assiduous study of Scripture and the fathers and became both a celebrated preacher (though none of his sermons was published) and a fervent Jansenist. This earned him the unwavering hostility of the Jesuits, who did all that they could to discredit him, and his life was far from easy. In 1653 he was sent to Rome to defend the Jansenist cause, and he did so on May 19 in the presence of Pope Innocent X himself. His presentation was subtle and skilled,[4] but by this time the Jan-

---

[2] *Description de l'Abbaye de La Trappe avec Constitutions*, 1. See Bell, *Rancé*, 288–89.

[3] The best account of Desmares's life and works, provided one can see through the anti-Jesuit bias, is to be found in [Abbé de La Croix], *Vies intéressantes et édifiantes des Religieuses de Port-Royal, et de plusieurs Personnes qui leur étoient attachées. Tome premier* ([Utrecht:] Aux dépens de la Compagnie, 1750), 457–96.

[4] See Louis-Gorin de Saint-Amour, *Journal de Mr de Saint-Amour, Docteur de Sorbonne, De ce qui c'est fait à Rome dans l'Affaire des Cinq Propositions* ([Amsterdam: L. & D. Elzevir,] 1662), 504–10, especially 508–10.

senist cause was effectively lost—the complicated and sometimes unsavory ecclesiastical politics need not concern us—and just twelve days later, on May 31, the pope issued the bull *Cum occasione*, which condemned five propositions supposedly found in the *Augustinus* of Cornelius Jansen, bishop of Ypres.[5]

As a consequence of this, when Desmares returned to France, he found himself the subject of a Jesuit manhunt, and there was the real possibility of his ending up in the Bastille. He therefore sought refuge with some old friends, namely, the duke and duchess of Liancourt (here is the link with the *Description*), whose country seat was to be found in Picardy, about thirty kilometres east of Beauvais. The duke was Roger Du Plessis de Liancourt, duke of La Roche-Guyon, and his wife was the former Jeanne de Schomberg, whom we shall meet again in a moment. She was two years younger than her husband, and both of them were Jansenist sympathizers. Their household at Liancourt was a sort of smaller version of Port-Royal, and offered sanctuary to those whose sympathies brought them into conflict with the orthodox establishment.

There is a charming story of Desmares meeting Louis XIV at Liancourt. The duke had presented the old man to the king, and Desmares said to Louis, "Sire, I would ask you a favor." "Ask it," said the king, "and I will grant it." "Permit me, sire," replied Desmares, "to put on my spectacles so that I may look upon and contemplate the countenance of my king."[6] Louis declared that of all the compliments he had ever received, none had pleased him more, and it certainly did no harm to Father Desmares. It was here, at Liancourt, with the king's permission, that he spent the rest of his days, and he died, aged eighty-seven, on January 19, 1687.

There can be little doubt that it was Desmares' close friendship with the duke and duchess and his residence at Liancourt

---

[5] Denzinger, nos. 2001–7.
[6] *Vies intéressantes et édifiantes*, 1:489.

that led to the suggestion that he was the author of the *Description*, but he did not write it. Desmares did have some publications to his credit—one of them, on the Council of Trent, was addressed to the duke of Liancourt[7]—but the *Description* is not among them. Not only does it not appear in any authoritative list of his writings,[8] but, as Professor Krailsheimer has pointed out, Desmares himself denied authorship.[9] The case is not in doubt. The author of the *Description*, as we said above, was undoubtedly André Félibien des Avaux, as is clearly stated in his obituary in the *Journal des Sçavans* for the year 1695:

> In 1670, in a letter to Madame the Duchess of Liancourt, he described the reform of the abbey of La Trappe and the holy life that was led there, something he had himself witnessed many times[10] over a period of seven or eight years. M. Colbert[11] had no sooner cast his eyes on this little work than M. Félibien presented him with a copy, and despite all his demanding responsibilities, he did not put it down until he had read

---

[7] *Vies intéressantes et édifiantes*, 1:490.

[8] See *Vies intéressantes et édifiantes*, 1:489–93; Louis Moréri, *Le grand dictionnaire historique, ou le mélange curieux de l'histoire sacrée et profane. Nouvelle édition. Tome quatrième* (Paris: Les Libraires Associés, 1759), 126–27.

[9] Alban J. Krailsheimer, *Armand-Jean de Rancé, Abbot of La Trappe: His Influence in the Cloister and the World* (Oxford: Clarendon Press, 1974), 85. See further Henri Tournoüer, *Bibliographie et iconographie de la Maison-Dieu Notre-Dame de La Trappe au diocèse de Sées, de Dom A.-I. Le Bouthillier de Rancé, Abbé et Réformateur de cette abbaye, et en général de tous les religieux du même monastère*, Documents sur la province du Perche, iv, 2 (Mortagne: Marchand & Gilles/Georges Meaux, 1894–1896), no. 139.

[10] According to Louis Dubois, *Histoire de l'abbé de Rancé et de sa réforme*, 2nd ed. (Paris: Poussielgue Frères, 1869), 1:396, Félibien visited La Trappe "more than ten times."

[11] Jean-Baptiste Colbert (1619–1683), Minister of Finance to Louis XIV from 1665 to 1683.

it from cover to cover. M. Félibien counted the marks of the esteem and friendship he had received over a period of fifty-five years from the abbot of La Trappe as one of the best things that had ever happened to him, [an abbot] who, after having governed this abbey so worthily for thirty-three years, has just resigned his office[12] in a rare example of humility, in order to complete in obedience a course that Heaven has filled with so many blessings and so many graces.[13]

André Félibien was born at Chartres in May 1619, and after completing his early education in that city, went to Paris at the age of fourteen to continue his studies. Here he was often to be seen at the town house of Catherine de Vivonne, marquise de Rambouillet—the *Hôtel de Rambouillet*—who presided over her fashionable *salon* for more than thirty years. Such *salons* cultivated purity, elegance, and beauty of language, polite manners, intelligence, and wit, and the subjects of conversation might include literature, religion, philosophy, art, politics, and, naturally, the most up-to-date gossip and talk of the town. In May 1647, when he was in his late twenties, Félibien was sent to Rome as secretary to the embassy of the ambassador extraordinary, François Duval, marquis of Fontenay-Mareuil. Here he stayed for two years, and here he met the great French

---

[12] Rancé resigned the abbacy in May 1695; Félibien died a few weeks later.

[13] *Journal des Sçavans* 23 (1695 [published in 1686]): 699–700. The obituary—pages 695 to 704—presents a very sound account of Félibien's life and works. See also André Fontaine, *Les Doctrines d'Art en France. Peintres, Amateurs, Critiques: De Poussin à Diderot* (Paris: Librairie Renouard—H. Laurens, éditeur, 1909), 41–60 (chap. II). Most comprehensive dictionaries of art, architecture, and the like contain brief notices of Félibien, but the only study wholly devoted to him is Stefan Germer, *Kunst, Macht, Diskurs: die intellektuelle Karriere des André Félibien im Frankreich von Louis XIV* (Munich: W. Fink, 1997), with an extensive bibliography on pages 525–53.

painter Nicolas Poussin, now back in Rome and at the height of his fame. In due course, he would publish a life of Poussin, a fine piece of work that still retains its value.[14] Whilst in the Holy City Félibien immersed himself in a study of its monuments and the literary treasures in its libraries, and when he returned to France in 1649 he immediately began work on what, in time, would be the ten volumes of his *Entretiens sur les Vies et les Ouvrages des plus excellents Peintures anciens et modernes* ("Conversations on the Lives and Works of the Most Eminent Painters, Ancient and Modern"), published between 1666 and 1688.[15]

Once back in France, Félibien married and settled in Paris, where his considerable talents were recognized by Nicolas Fouquet, minister of finance under Louis XIV, and, after Fouquet's fall from grace and subsequent imprisonment, by his successor Jean-Baptiste Colbert, to whom, as we saw above, Félibien presented a copy of his *Description*. In February 1663 Colbert had founded the *Académie des Inscriptions et Belles-Lettres*, with Félibien as one of its earliest members, and Colbert's patronage continued with Félibien's appointment, three years later, as official Court Historian—*Historiographe du Roi*—to Louis XIV. It will hardly come as a surprise to find him appointed secretary, at the very end of 1671, to the newly established *Académie royale d'architecture*, founded by Louis at the instigation, yet again, of Colbert, and other honors followed.

Félibien was a prolific writer, and apart from his *Entretiens* published a number of important works on art and architecture. His *Des principes de l'architecture, de la sculpture, de la peinture, et des autres arts qui en dépendent. Avec un Dictionnaire des*

---

[14] See Claire Pace, *Félibien's Life of Poussin* (London: A. Zwemmer, 1981).

[15] See Ugo Dionne, "Félibien dialoguiste: les *Entretiens sur les vies des peintres*," *Dix-septième siècle*, no. 210 (2001): 49–74.

Termes propres à chacun de ces Arts ("On the Principles of Architecture, Sculpture, Painting, and Other Arts Dependent on Them, with a Dictionary of Terms Proper to Each Art") was published in 1676, and it was Félibien who was primarily responsible for laying the rational foundations for the modern disciplines of art history and art criticism. His religious sensibilities are revealed in his translation of the *Interior Castle* of Saint Teresa of Avila, published at Paris in 1670,[16] and his numerous journeys to La Trappe. He died in Paris on June 11, 1695, and was survived by five children, three boys and two girls. Of the three sons, the eldest became a canon and dean of the Cathedral of Bourges, but it was the second and third who followed most closely in their father's footsteps. Jean-François Félibien was treasurer of the *Académie des Inscriptions et Belles-Lettres*, *Historiographe du Roi*, and secretary to the *Académie royale d'architecture*, and his younger brother, Michel, echoed his father's piety by becoming a monk of the Congregation of Saint-Maur at the abbey of Saint-Germain-des-Prés in Paris. Both were authors in their own right and left behind historical and architectural works of considerable merit.

Félibien's *Description de l'abbaye de La Trappe* was not the only work of its kind. People were fascinated by the austerity of life at the abbey and by the story of the dramatic conversion of its celebrated abbot. But according to Louis Dubois, Félibien's description was "the best and most complete" of them all.[17] Dubois also tells us that the *Description* was translated into English and that this translation was widely read in England.[18] There was indeed a tradition that the work had been translated by the Scottish statesman and Jacobite, James Drummond, fourth earl and first duke of Perth. Born in 1648, he had a

---

[16] *Le Chateau intérieur, ou les Demeures de l'âme, composé par sainte Thérèse de Jésus* (Paris: F. Léonard, 1671).

[17] Dubois, *Rancé*, 1:395.

[18] Dubois, *Rancé*, 1:395.

distinguished political career, culminating in his appointment as lord chancellor of Scotland from 1684 to 1688. In 1685 he and his brother had converted to Roman Catholicism, and the next year opened a Catholic chapel in Edinburgh (their attendance there caused a riot). The earl then gave his wholehearted support to the Catholic king James II, but when James was overthrown in the Revolution of 1688—the so-called Glorious Revolution—Drummond was imprisoned. He was not released until August 1693, and only then if he undertook to leave Britain. He joined his exiled king at the château of Saint-Germain-en-Laye on the outskirts of Paris, where he was appointed tutor to the young prince of Wales, and went on to have as distinguished a career in France as he had enjoyed in Scotland. James died on September 16, 1701, and Drummond survived him for some fifteen years, all of them spent in exile. He himself died on May 11, 1716, and was buried in the chapel of the Scots College in Paris.[19]

James first visited La Trappe on November 24, 1690, began a correspondence with Rancé, and returned to visit the abbey a number of times thereafter.[20] It is perfectly possible that he was accompanied by James Drummond, and it is equally possible that the earl did indeed translate Félibien's *Description*. But Professor Krailsheimer tells us that "I have been unable to authenticate the story of his alleged translation,"[21] and despite assiduous searching I have found no trace of it myself. If there was a translation, it appears never to have been printed, though it is not impossible that it once existed—and perhaps still exists—in manuscript. But I fear we must take with a grain

---

[19] At what is now 65, rue du Cardinal-Lemoine. Until 1793 the college was part of the University of Paris and is now the home of the Association Franco-Écossais. The duke's memorial may still be seen in the chapel on the second floor.
[20] See Krailsheimer, *Rancé*, 265–71; Rancé, *Correspondance*, 4:599.
[21] Krailsheimer, *Rancé*, 86 n. 2.

of salt Dubois' assertion that Drummond's translation was widely read in England. So far as I know, the present translation is the first in that language. Let us now turn our attention to the recipient of Félibien's *Description*, its "onlie begetter," the importunate noble lady who gave him no peace until he took pen in hand and provided her with what she sought.

The Duchess of Liancourt

Henri de Schomberg, count of Nanteuil-le-Haudouin and Durtal, duke of Alluyn, was born at Paris in 1575. The Schombergs were of ancient stock, and members of the family had held important positions in a number of German principalities, especially Saxony. Henri de Schomberg enjoyed a distinguished military career, as a result of which he was promoted by Louis XIII to the rank of marshal of France in 1625. His most celebrated achievement was his defeat of the English forces under George Villiers, first duke of Buckingham, at the siege of La Rochelle, an engagement in which Villiers lost more than half his army. Some years later, in 1632, he defeated the forces of Henri II de Montmorency at the battle of Castelnaudary, and after Montmorency's subsequent execution was rewarded with the governorship of the Languedoc, formerly held by Montmorency. He did not, however, live long to enjoy it, for he died of apoplexy a few weeks later on November 17, 1632.

Meanwhile, in 1598, when he was in his early twenties, Henri had married Françoise d'Espinay, the daughter of Claude, marquis d'Espinay, and the couple had two children, a son and a daughter, before Françoise's untimely death in January 1602. The son was Charles de Schomberg and the daughter Jeanne de Schomberg, to whom Félibien addressed his *Description de l'abbaye de La Trappe*.[22] A year before his own

---

[22] The only full-length study of Jeanne de Schomberg and the château of Liancourt is a rather odd book (entirely without source

death the marshal married again, and his wife bore him a posthumous daughter, Jeanne-Armande de Schomberg, whose eventful life is not here our concern.

Jeanne de Schomberg grew up to be an intelligent, well-educated, and attractive woman, tall and dark-haired, very devout, and with a high sense of morality. Her sense of morality, in time, would lead her to sympathize with the Jansenists and the Solitaries of Port-Royal. In April 1618 a marriage was arranged between Jeanne and François de Cossé, duke of Brissac, but although this was certainly a good match for the noble families involved, it was a disaster for Jeanne de Schomberg. She and her new husband were wholly incompatible, and the following year their marriage was annulled on the dubious grounds of impotence. Meanwhile, Jeanne had met Roger Du Plessis, duke of Liancourt and La Roche-Guyon, who was the son of Charles Du Plessis, first equerry to Henri III and governor of Metz, and his wife Antoinette de Pons, marquise of Guercheville. The two were certainly attracted to each other (by no means a necessary requisite for a successful marriage in seventeenth-century France) and were married on February 14, 1620. The groom was two years older than the bride.

Roger Du Plessis was a handsome young man with—alas!—an eye for the ladies. Despite his affection for his wife, he was not averse to finding pleasure elsewhere, and his lighthearted conduct and various affairs caused his pious and devout spouse much heartache. She, for her part, tried to lure him back by rebuilding and refurbishing the family château at Liancourt, not far from Beauvais, and, above all, by planning and planting the magnificent gardens that were the glory of Liancourt and enlivening their beauty by means of waterways

---

references, but a good read) written by a rather odd man: Xavier de Courville, *Liancourt: sa dame et ses jardins* (Paris: Bloud & Gay, 1925; repr. Paris: Le Livre d'histoire, 2004). Xavier de Courville died in 1984.

and fountains that, it is said, were the inspiration for Versailles. For many years, Jeanne's efforts did not meet with great success, but then the duke contracted smallpox, a very dangerous disease in seventeenth-century France and often fatal. Jeanne became his nurse and never left his side, and when the duke fortunately recovered, he was not the man he had been. Not long afterwards Jeanne herself fell seriously ill, and her husband, now well on his way to becoming a reformed person, cared for her with the same devotion she had shown to him. And when she, too, recovered, their lives were never the same.

Like Rancé, Roger Du Plessis had undergone a conversion. It might not have been quite so intense or quite so dramatic as that of the abbot of La Trappe, but it was a true conversion nevertheless. He adopted much of the life of a penitent, and he and his wife established close contacts with the Jansenists and semi-Jansenists of Port-Royal des Champs. The couple also made munificent donations to the abbey, and, as Mary Schimmelpenninck tells us, "M. de Liancourt erected a large range of buildings in the court, for the reception of those guests, whose piety led them to renew their strength, by a temporary seclusion among the inmates of Port Royal."[23]

As we have already mentioned, Liancourt itself became a refuge for those persecuted for their Jansenist sympathies—Toussaint-Guy-Joseph Desmares was one of them—and the duke and duchess spent their days in pious exercises and good works. They had but one child, Henri-Roger Du Plessis-Liancourt, count of La Roche-Guyon, who was killed in his twenties at the siege of Mardick in Flanders. He had married Anne-Élisabeth de Lannoy, and they had one daughter, Jeanne-Charlotte Du Plessis-Liancourt, mademoiselle de La Roche-Guyon, who, at the age of nine, was sent for her education to

---

[23] Mary A. Schimmelpenninck, *Select Memoirs of Port Royal*, 4th ed. (London: Hamilton, Adams, & Co., 1835), 1:186. The duke also had his own *pied-à-terre* at Port-Royal.

Port-Royal, and for whom her grandmother, Jeanne de Schomberg, wrote the *Règlement donné par une dame de haute qualité à M*** sa petite-fille, pour sa conduite, et pour celle de sa maison*,[24] published after her death by the abbé Jean-Jacques Boileau in 1698. The duchess herself had died on June 14, 1674, and was survived by her devoted husband for no more than a few weeks. He died on August 1 of the same year. She was seventy-four and he seventy-six.

It was for this talented and devout woman that Félibien wrote his description of La Trappe. There is no record of any correspondence between Jeanne de Schomberg and Rancé, but given her background and her sympathies, it is perfectly understandable that she would have had a deep interest in the abbey and in the strict reforms that had been carried out there by its celebrated abbot. Let us therefore give a brief account of abbey and abbot, since not all that Félibien tells us is quite accurate.

La Trappe and Rancé

William the Conqueror, William I of England, had four sons: Robert, Richard, William, and Henry. He also had at least five daughters, but since they could not inherit the throne, they are not here our concern. Richard, the second son, died before his father, and on William I's death in 1087, William II, William Rufus, inherited the crown of England, and Robert, Robert Curthose, inherited his father's possessions in Normandy. Henry inherited hardly anything but managed to buy certain estates on and around the Cherbourg Peninsula in western Normandy from his brother. Then, when William Rufus met his untimely death in 1100 while hunting in the New Forest

---

[24] The most recent edition is that by Collette H. Winn in the series Textes de la Renaissance. Série l'éducation féminine de la Renaissance à l'âge classique, 15 (Paris: Honoré Champion, 1997).

(conspiracy theories abound here, some of them very strange), Henry seized the English throne. Robert, who refused to recognize Henry's kingship, invaded England in 1101, but the invasion was unsuccessful, and Robert was forced into a short-lived negotiated peace with his brother. The peace came to an end in 1104 and 1105 when Henry invaded Normandy and, on September 28, 1106, won a decisive victory against Robert at the Battle of Tinchebray. Robert was captured and spent the rest of his days in prison, first in England and then in Wales.

Henry now claimed Normandy for the English throne, but his claim—as we might expect—was not unopposed. It was challenged by Louis VI of France, Baldwin of Flanders, and Fulk of Anjou, who supported the claims of Robert's son, and between 1116 and 1119 there was a series of rebellions in the region claimed by Henry. The last of these took place in 1119 when Louis VI came down the Seine and invaded Henry's lands, and the opposing armies met at the Battle of Brémule on August 20, 1119. After a series of ill-coordinated cavalry charges by the French, the English and Normans won the field and the French army fled in disarray. Normandy was now part of Henry's realm, and in 1120 Louis had no choice but to negotiate a favorable peace.

Following his short and successful campaign, Henry and his entourage made preparations to return to England, the king in one vessel and his only legitimate son, William the Aetheling, in another, the White Ship. William was to be accompanied by about three hundred passengers, most of whom were noble and wealthy landowners, and one of these passengers was Matilda, countess of the Perche, who was William's half sister and the wife of Rotrou III, count of Mortagne and lord of Nogent.

The White Ship was due to sail from Barfleur on November 25, 1120, but its scheduled departure was delayed as a result of a riotous farewell party, and it was twilight before the ship finally set sail. The result, alas, was tragedy. A drunken helmsman ran the ship aground on the *Coste raze*, a dangerous rock just outside Barfleur, and it immediately began to sink. William was saved by his guards and rowed away from the wreck, but when he heard his half sister Matilda crying out for help on the sinking ship, he straightaway went to her assistance. It was an unwise move. Those in the water tried to clamber into the prince's small boat, the boat capsized, and both Matilda and the heir to the English throne vanished beneath the cold waters of the English Channel.[25]

When the news of the disaster came to Rotrou in Normandy, he mourned the death of his wife and resolved to build a memorial chapel for the repose of her soul. He chose a location not far from Mortagne, and the chapel, dedicated to Our Lady, appears to have been consecrated in 1122.[26] The site of the chapel, on the western edge of the forest of the Perche, "in a deep valley, isolated and wild, covered with lakes,"[27] was known as La Trappe, a term associated with the chase.[28]

Some time later (the date is uncertain) Rotrou invited six monks from the Savigniac abbey of Breuil-Benoît, situated not far from the Perche, to come to the site and transform it into a proper religious house. This invitation could not have been delivered before 1137, the date of the foundation of Breuil-Benoît, and the date usually cited for the foundation of the new abbey is December 2, 1140, when Rotrou made a formal

---

[25] The main narrative sources for the wreck of the White Ship are William of Malmesbury, Henry of Huntingdon, Eadmer, and Orderic Vitalis. For bibliographical details, see Wilfred L. Warren, *Henry II* (Berkeley/Los Angeles: University of California Press, 1973), 3 n. 1.

[26] See the *Memoriale fundationis hujus abbatiæ* in Dubois, *Histoire*, 285.

[27] Dubois, *Histoire*, 21.

[28] For a long (and not always quite accurate) discussion of the etymology of the name, see Charencey, 1:46–50.

donation of land to La Trappe.[29] The donation was confirmed by Rotrou IV in 1189, who added further donations of his own.[30] By 1189, however, La Trappe had become a Cistercian house (the Savigniacs had amalgamated with the Cistercians in 1147), and the abbey had entered upon a period of flourishing prosperity, governed for an astonishing fifty-four years, from 1189 to 1243,[31] by abbot Adam Gauthier, an effective, intelligent, and far-seeing administrator. During this period, La Trappe received yet more donations, primarily in Normandy, and under Gauthier's guiding hand the monastery was considerably enlarged, and a new or rebuilt church was dedicated to the Virgin by Robert III Le Baube, archbishop of Rouen, on April 27, 1214. The bishops of Evreux and Séez assisted at the ceremony, and it was attended by Thomas I, count of the Perche (the great-grandson of the founder), together with a host of dignitaries.[32] During the same period, the abbey was taken under the protection of the Holy See by popes Eugenius III, Alexander III, Innocent III, and Honorius III,[33] and in September 1246 it was taken under the protection of King Louis IX, who confirmed its possessions, rights, and privileges while adding others of his own.[34]

The period of prosperity was not to last. With the beginning of the Hundred Years' War in 1337, Normandy was a focus of military operations, and the countryside was regularly ravaged

---

[29] The *Memoriale* gives the date as the fourth day before the Nones of December 1140, which is December 2. Charencey, 1:52, mistakenly gives December 10, which is the fourth day before the Ides of December.

[30] See Dubois, *Histoire*, 294–99 (Pièce justificative, no. 2).

[31] Charencey, 1:73–92.

[32] Charencey, 1:90.

[33] Dubois, *Histoire*, 23, 300–11 (Pièces justificatives, nos. III–VII).

[34] Dubois, *Histoire*, 23–24, 312–13 (Pièce justificative, no. VIII). There are, however, certain historical problems with this document: see *L'Abbaye de La Trappe*, 31.

by armed bands intent on pillage and destruction. The abbey was plundered in 1361, and the monks were forced to seek refuge in the nearby château of Bonsmoulins, where they remained for two years.[35] During a temporary lull in hostilities under Charles V they were able to return to their abbey, but the shaky peace was not to last. In 1376 La Trappe was again attacked by the English, and much of it was burned. Almost all the charters were destroyed, and of all the major monastic buildings only the church and chapter house were spared.[36] Again there came a period of unstable calm, but hostilities then broke out anew, and in 1417 the monks were again forced to flee. They were absent from their abbey for more than thirty years, and when they returned in 1449 they found only ruined buildings, hardly habitable. Their attempts at reconstruction were severely hampered by the troubled conditions of the times, and in 1469 the abbey was vandalized yet again, and both church and archives were pillaged.

Robert III Lavolle, under whose abbacy this vandalism occurred, either resigned or was forced to resign in 1476,[37] and he was succeeded by Henri Hohart or Hoart, but only after an unpleasant and unseemly legal battle had been fought between Hohart and a rival candidate.[38] Hohart himself was much occupied with rebuilding the structures that had been destroyed during the Hundred Years' War, and eventually resigned the abbacy in 1518. He died two years later. He was followed by the last of the regular abbots, Robert IV Ravey (1518–1527), the former procurator of the abbey, who resigned, blind and infirm, in April 1527. The monks of La Trappe then elected Julien des Noës, who, like his predecessor, had also been procurator of the abbey, but the king, Francis I, refused to ratify the election. The monks therefore reelected Julien in May 1528, and,

---

[35] Charencey, 1:130.
[36] Charencey, 1:131.
[37] Charencey, 1:138.
[38] Charencey, 1:138.

once again, the king refused his consent.[39] Instead he imposed on the unwilling monks the first of a series of commendatory abbots, in this case the humanist, poet, and diplomat Jean du Bellay, friend and counsellor of the king, bishop of Bayonne in 1532, bishop of Paris from 1532 to 1551, and cardinal from May 21, 1535.[40]

Commendatory abbots rarely lived in their monasteries, and even if they wished to do so, their other duties rarely allowed it. Many commendatory abbots, therefore, were no more than absentee landlords whose main interest was the collection of as large a portion of the monastic revenues as might fall into their purse. The consequences were inevitable. The Divine Office was neglected, buildings fell into disrepair, monastic populations diminished, and monastic discipline became a mere shadow of what it once had been. Both the Fifth Lateran Council (1514) and the Council of Trent (1545–1563) called for the abolition of the system, but it was too deeply entrenched, and by the end of the sixteenth century the great majority of Cistercian abbeys in France—La Trappe among them—were held *in commendam*. At La Trappe this lamentable period would come to an end only in 1664, when Armand-Jean de Rancé entered the monastery as its regular abbot.

He was born at Paris on January 9, 1626, and was one of a number of children.[41] His parents, Denis Bouthillier and Charlotte Joly, were well to do and enjoyed the favor of Cardinal Richelieu, who was Rancé's godfather. Rancé was christened Armand-Jean in honour of his illustrious patron. Rancé's elder brother, Denis-François, was six years older than Armand-Jean but had never enjoyed good health, and he died

---

[39] Charencey, 1:140–41.

[40] The beginning of du Bellay's abbacy is sometimes dated to 1526 (as in, for example, *L'Abbaye de La Trappe*, 33–34), but the actual date appears to be May 1528 (see Charencey, 1:140).

[41] For Rancé's life, works, and influence, see Krailsheimer, *Rancé*; Krailsheimer, *Legacy*; and Bell, *Rancé*.

in 1637 at the age of seventeen. He had been destined for the church, just as his younger brother had been destined to have become a knight of Malta, but on his death, the young Rancé stepped into his ecclesiastical shoes and found himself commendatory superior of five religious houses, one of which was the dilapidated abbey of La Trappe in the wilds of Normandy.[42]

Armand-Jean had begun his education at home, under the guidance of private tutors[43] (a common practice at the time), and was clearly an attentive and intelligent pupil. At the age of thirteen he published a commentary on the Greek poet Anacreon and dedicated it, with a letter in Greek, to his godfather Cardinal Richelieu.[44] That was in 1639; two years before this Rancé's father had bought a country estate at Véretz, not far from Tours.[45] Rancé would come to know and love it. But then, in October 1639 his mother died, to Rancé's great sorrow, and in about 1642 the young boy, now in his teens, entered the Collège de Harcourt of the University of Paris to complete his education. His studies were primarily classical, philosophical, and theological, and after he took his MA degree in 1644,[46] he began to make his way in society. One of the noble families with which he became acquainted was the house of Montbazon, and he became even more intimately acquainted with the lady of the house, the beautiful Marie d'Avaugour de Bretagne,

---

[42] See n. 21 to the translation.

[43] The best known is Jean Favier, who remained a lifelong friend and correspondent. The letters cited at nn. 83 and 84 below were addressed to Favier. See further Élie Jaloustre, *Un précepteur auvergnat de l'abbé de Rancé* (Clermont-Ferrand: G. Mont-Louis, 1887). This is an excellent study of a remarkable man.

[44] See Bell, *Rancé*, 253–55, 286.

[45] For a full description and detailed history of the estate, see Louis Bossebœuf, *Le Chateau de Véretz: son histoire et ses souvenirs* (Tours: Imprimerie Tourangelle, 1903).

[46] Not in 1643, as appears in Krailsheimer, *Rancé*, 6. See Bell, *Library*, 21 n. 20.

Madame de Montbazon, who, it was said, had the most welcoming bed in France.[47]

In 1648 Rancé was ordained to the diaconate and in 1651 to the priesthood, by which time he was head of the family. His father had died in 1650, and Rancé had inherited the country estate at Véretz. By 1654 he was a doctor of theology and the following year was sent by his uncle, the archbishop of Tours, as a delegate to the General Assembly of the Clergy of France. Here he acquitted himself competently, if not brilliantly, but he found the whole proceeding intensely boring, and before it had ended he had discreetly slipped away and retreated to his beloved Véretz. Life as a country squire clearly appealed to him (he adored hunting and was a superb horseman), and his days at Véretz were made yet more enjoyable by visits from his mistress, Madame de Montbazon. But in April 1657, the duchess contracted *la rougeole*, which was either measles or scarlet fever (no doctor at the time could have distinguished between them), and both were far more dangerous then than they are now. A few days later she was dead.

We now come to the gruesome story of the duchess's severed head. In 1685 Daniel de Larroque had published a scurrilous attack on Rancé with the title *Les véritables motifs de la conversion de l'abbé de Rancé, avec quelques réflexions sur sa vie et sur ses écrits* ("The True Motives for the Conversion of the Abbé de Rancé, with Some Reflections on his Life and Writings"), a book in which Rancé is portrayed as proud, vain, self-centered, and ambitious.[48] According to Larroque, one of the main motives for Rancé's conversion was his ghastly discovery of the headless body of his adored mistress, for he had been at Véretz at the time of her death, and although his servants knew of her decease, they had concealed it from him. When, therefore, Rancé returned to Paris,

---

[47] On the life and character of Madame de Montbazon, see Bell, *Rancé*, 176–90.
[48] See Bell, *Rancé*, 147–66.

he went straight up to the duchess's chamber, which he was permitted to enter at any time, but instead of the pleasures he had anticipated, the first thing he saw was her coffin. That it awaited his mistress was obvious, for he was confronted with the sight of her head, all covered with blood, which had accidentally rolled from under a cloth that had been carelessly thrown over it. It had been severed from the body at the neck [by the undertakers] so as to avoid the need to make a new and longer coffin. The one that had been prepared had been so poorly measured that it was six inches too short.[49]

I have shown elsewhere that this story is a fabrication,[50] but a fabrication that might be based on fact. Given her age and her sudden and unexpected death, it is probable that Madame de Montbazon's body had been autopsied; at that time autopsies were regularly performed in the house of the deceased, and the removal of the head was a standard accompaniment to the opening of the body.[51] It is quite possible, then, that by some hideous mischance, Rancé had indeed stumbled upon the headless and eviscerated corpse of the woman he loved, though Larroque's tale of the incompetent undertakers may safely be dismissed.

Whatever actually happened, the death of Madame de Montbazon was the last and most terrible event in a succession of circumstances, and after her decease Rancé withdrew to Véretz and began to take the first definite steps on the path

---

[49] Daniel de Larroque, *Les véritables motifs de la conversion de l'abbé de Rancé, avec quelques réflexions sur sa vie et sur ses écrits, ou Les Entretiens de Timocrate et de Philandre sur un livre qui a pour titre, Les s. devoirs de la vie monastique* (Cologne: P. Marteau, 1685), 27–28.

[50] See David N. Bell, "Daniel de Larroque, Armand-Jean de Rancé, and the Head of Madame de Montbazon," *Cîteaux—Commentarii cistercienses* 53 (2002): 305–31.

[51] See Bell, "Daniel de Larroque," 312–14.

that would lead him from the fashionable world of Paris and the delights of his country estate to the poverty, austerity, and mortifications of La Trappe. It took him some six years, and many consultations with many people, to come to a final decision, and in the spring of 1658 he set off on a tour of those religious houses of which he was commendatory superior. A second tour followed in 1659—Rancé was still unsure of what to do and where to go—but by 1660 he had begun to see clearly that, whether he liked it or not, God was calling him to the monastic life. And so, over the next two years, he divested himself of all his benefices save La Trappe, sold his beloved Véretz, and in August 1662 asked the authorities of the Cistercian Strict Observance to send a few monks from the Strict Observance monastery of Perseigne to the run-down abbey of La Trappe, which housed, at the time, only six monks and one lay brother.[52]

What was the abbey like at this time? It was, quite simply, almost entirely a ruin. Doors were open day and night, the entrance hall was filthy, access to the upper story, where the floorboards were rotten, was by means of a rickety ladder, the cloister had lost its columns and its roof, the parlor was now a stable, the refectory was used as a bowling alley, the dormitory housed only nightbirds, the archives were scattered all over the floor, and in the church one saw only broken pavement, fallen stones, ruin, filth, and cobwebs. The walls were ready to collapse and the bell tower ready to fall. The monks slept where they could, and the commendatory abbot's bailiff, with his whole family, lodged with them.[53]

Rancé himself went to La Trappe to oversee the essential work of rebuilding and restoration and stayed there from

---

[52] See nn. 22 and 54 to the translation.

[53] This is a summary of part of Dom Dominique Georges' *procès-verbal* submitted to the general chapter in 1686. For a complete translation, see Bell, *Library*, 8–9. For Dom Dominique Georges, see n. 46 to the translation.

September 1662 to January 1663. These few months seem to have provided him with final confirmation that he was treading the right path, for him the only path, and on June 13, 1663, he took the habit as a novice at Perseigne. At that time a year's novitiate was standard, and for Rancé the year was hard and demanding. His health broke down in October (he was forced to return to La Trappe for a while to recuperate), but when the year was finally over, he received the abbatial benediction on July 13, 1664, and entered La Trappe as its regular abbot the next day.[54]

He had been there only a few weeks when he was sent to Rome to defend the cause of the Strict Observance—Félibien mentions this in his *Description*[55]—but he did not enjoy his time in the Holy City. Nor was the Roman mission a success, and after Rancé returned to La Trappe in May 1666, that was where he would stay. Save for short trips on official business, he never left the abbey again. It cannot be said that he had an easy abbacy. He was a man who had an unfortunate gift for making enemies (though his monks adored him), and the years from 1666 to about 1675 were riven by struggles with those opposed to the reform, strained relationships with his own superiors in the Strict Observance, and a number of bitter controversies with Guillaume Le Roy, commendatory abbot of Hautefontaine, on the question of humiliations; with Dom Innocent Le Masson, general of the Carthusians, on the question as to whether the Carthusians could justly be accused of laxity; and with the learned Maurist Dom Jean Mabillon, ever the gentleman, on the matter of monastic studies.[56]

---

[54] See nn. 37–40 to the translation. Félibien has the wrong date for Rancé's abbatial benediction, but it is no more than a slip of the pen or a misreading by the printer: *trois* for *treize*.

[55] See nn. 44–51 to the translation.

[56] See, briefly, Bell, *Rancé*, 111–14, 145–47. We will say more on the controversy over humiliations in a moment.

As Félibien makes clear, running the abbey was a time-consuming operation, and Rancé took part in almost everything. As the abbey grew in numbers,[57] the demands on its abbot increased, and even Rancé's iron constitution began to give way under the strain. By 1694 he was suffering severely from rheumatism, perhaps rheumatoid arthritis, and was having trouble with breathing and digestion. He had no choice but to enter the infirmary, and the next year, in May 1695, he resigned the abbacy and was succeeded as abbot by Dom Zozime Foisil. Dom Zozime, however, administered the house for only three months before he died, quite unexpectedly, in March 1696. He in turn was succeeded by Dom Armand-François Gervaise, a turbulent priest who deserves a study of his own. Gervaise was forced to resign in 1698, and the governance of the abbey passed into the hands of Dom Jacques de La Cour. It was during his abbacy that Rancé himself died. By September 1700 he had to be carried to Mass; his body was shrunken, he could breathe only with great difficulty, and he could find no comfortable place to lie. "On whichever side he lay," says Dubois, "he seemed to be lying on thorns that pierced his flesh."[58] He was still perfectly lucid, however, and remained lucid until he died on October 27, 1700, between one and two o'clock in the afternoon. He was seventy-four.

When the first edition of Félibien's *Description* was published in 1671, Rancé had been abbot of La Trappe for seven years, and it was in precisely that year that we see the first traces of his conflict with his former friend Guillaume Le Roy. Le Roy had spent time with Rancé at Véretz shortly before he sold the estate and had been welcomed at La Trappe in June 1671. But what he saw there, and what he misinterpreted as

---

[57] On the increase in the monastic population at La Trappe, see n. 53 to the translation.
[58] Dubois, *Rancé*, 1:558.

Rancé's teaching on deliberate humiliations,[59] led to his writing a *Dissertation* on the subject; Rancé responded to this in 1677 with his *Lettre d'un abbé régulier sur le sujet des humiliations, et autres pratiques de religion* ("Letter of a Regular Abbot on the Subject of Humiliations, and Other Practices of the Religious Life").[60] It is, alas, a scathing and intemperate letter, cutting and resentful, and Rancé had not wished it published. When it was published, against his wishes, he wrote to Le Roy to offer his apologies. "The fault I committed," he wrote,

> was to communicate [the letter] to a person who made a copy of it, and who did not preserve the secrecy and fidelity he owed me. It is difficult to imagine that your own *Dissertation* will not meet with a similar end any day, since it is now in the hands of so many people. I have no solution for this, save to be patient and resign myself to suffering the mortification I feel. The Father Abbot of Châtillon[61] will doubtless have told you, Monsieur, how this happened, and the just cause I have for complaint against the one who divulged the letter. It would serve no purpose to tell you the whole story. I will only state that my *grief*[62] at this unfortunate event could not be greater, and that if it had been in my power to suppress the letter and all the copies, no one would ever have heard anything of it. I beg you most humbly to be convinced of this, and believe me

---

[59] See Rancé, *Correspondance*, 1:476–79 (Letter 720718), and n. 109 to the translation.

[60] See Bell, *Rancé*, 296–97.

[61] Claude Le Maître, prior of Hautefontaine and then abbot of Châtillon from 1669 to 1693. He became abbot when his predecessor Jacques Minguet resigned and entered La Trappe. Minguet's story is told at some length in the 1689 edition of Félibien's description and translated in full below. Le Maître was a trusted friend of both Rancé and Le Roy.

[62] The word (*la douleur*) is underlined in the original.

to be, with all esteem and every consideration possible, your humble and most obedient servant.[63]

Who was the source of the leak? Who was it who did not preserve the secrecy and fidelity he owed to the abbot? It was almost certainly none other than André Félibien, the author of the *Description*, which, we might add, was also published without Rancé's approval. There can be no doubt that he leaked it with the best of intentions, but it simply exacerbated an already unpleasant situation, and Rancé's apology to Le Roy did no good.[64] The bitter conflict dragged on for years. Félibien's indiscretion may also be seen in the publication of the "Historical Account of the Constitutions of the Abbey of Our Lady of La Trappe," which comprises the second part of the 1689 edition of the *Description*, and it is to an examination of those Constitutions—what they were and where they came from—that we must now turn our attention.

The Constitutions and Regulations of La Trappe

Let us begin by comparing the two main editions of the *Description*, the first edition of 1671 and the new edition of 1689. Both were published as neat duodecimos—the favorite format of the seventeenth century—and both are fairly brief. The 1671 edition bears the title *Description de l'abbaye de La Trappe* and was published by Frédéric Léonard, "Imprimeur ordinaire du Roy, ruë Saint Jacques, à l'Escu de Venise," at Paris. The description begins immediately on page 3 (there is no preliminary matter) and ends on page 139. The text is followed by four pages, unpaginated, of the *Privilège du Roy* and the date of the first printing, February 9, 1671. The new edition

---

[63] Rancé, *Correspondance*, 2:133 (Letter 770414).

[64] It is probable that Félibien was also involved in the scheme to force Rancé to print his *De la sainteté et des devoirs de la vie monastique*: see Krailsheimer, *Rancé*, 44.

of 1689 is entitled *Description de l'abbaye de La Trape. Nouvelle Édition. Avec Figures,* and was published by Jacques Le Febvre, "au dernier Pillier de la grand'Salle du Palais, à côté des Eaux & Forêts," also at Paris. In the first edition, La Trappe has two P's, in the new edition, one. The 1689 edition begins with an unpaginated letter from "The Bookseller to the Reader" (translated below), then an *Extrait du Privilège du Roy* with the date of the first printing, November 29, 1698, then a "Summary of the Book," and then the text itself, beginning on page 1 and ending on page 216. The two figures are a plan of the abbey and a view of the interior of the church. Both are reproduced below.

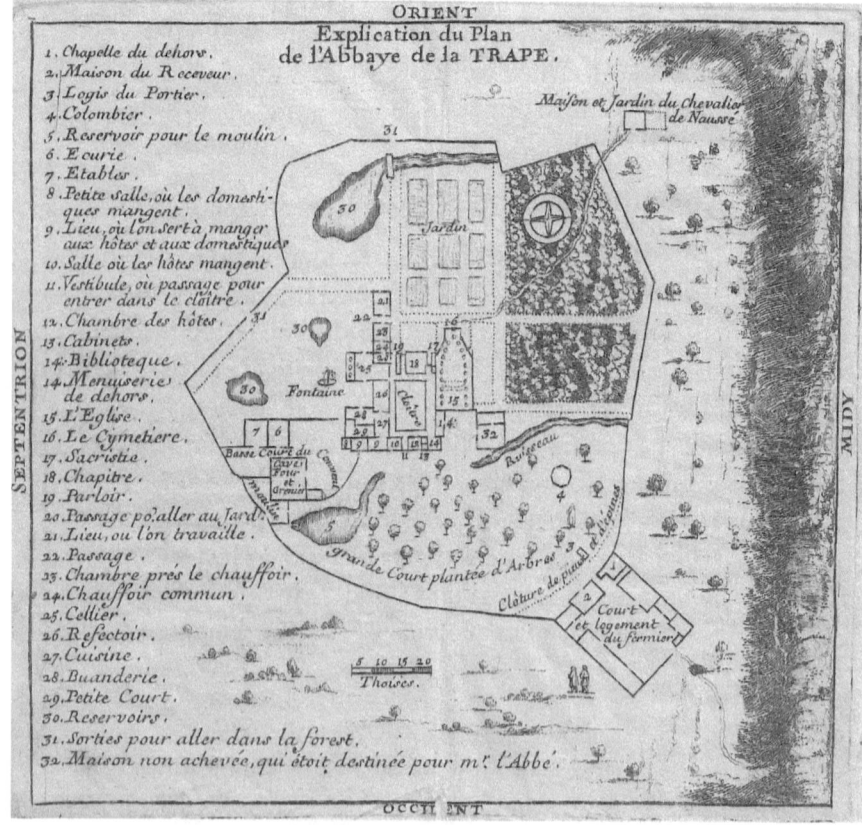

Figure 1. Plan of the Abbey of La Trappe, with east at the top.

Figure 2. The interior of the Church of La Trappe.

What are the differences between the two editions? They are of three types. First, there are numerous differences in spelling and the correction of an occasional typographical error. Nothing here is of any consequence, for although French orthography in the seventeenth century was well on its way to standardization, it had not yet arrived. Second, there are two corrections to the 1671 edition, and one update. The corrections are (i) the date at which Rancé left La Trappe for Rome: the incorrect 19 September of the 1671 edition has been corrected to 9 September in the new edition,[65] and (ii) the time at which the monks finish their reading after Sext has been corrected from half-past two to half-past ten.[66] The update pertains to the monastic population of La Trappe. In 1671, says Félibien, there were "more than forty" religious at the abbey; by 1689 this number has increased to "more than a hundred," though this may be somewhat exaggerated.[67] On the other hand, there are three statements in the 1671 edition that we might have expected to be corrected or updated in 1689 but that, in fact, are not. The first is the date of Rancé's abbatial blessing. This took place on July 13, 1664—the date is not in doubt—but both the 1671 and 1689 editions have July 3.[68] The second is Félibien's statement in the 1671 edition that "Since the time that Monsieur l'Abbé [de Rancé] undertook the reform of this abbey [i.e., in July 1664] there have been the deaths of only one Brother Oblate and one Professed Monk."[69] Exactly the same sentence occurs in the 1689 edition,[70] but by that time it was certainly wrong. By 1689 there had been very many deaths at La Trappe, and the mortality of the monks was common talk

---

[65] See n. 49 to the translation.
[66] See n. 91 to the translation.
[67] See n. 53 to the translation.
[68] See n. 37 to the translation.
[69] Pages 109–10 of the 1671 edition.
[70] Page 97 of the 1689 edition.

outside the abbey.⁷¹ And the third is the statement on page 80 of the 1671 edition that most of the twelve or thirteen novices at the abbey at that time were priests, and that some of them were more than fifty years old. This statement remains unchanged in the new edition of 1689.⁷²

The third and most important difference between the two editions is the additions. There are four of these. The first, of least consequence, is the addition of marginal subtitles, which are reproduced, with the appropriate page numbers, in the *Sommaire du Livre* at the beginning of the book. The second, of more importance, is the paragraph telling the story of the lodging (*logement*) that Rancé intended to have built for himself by the side of the church but which, because of his responsibilities for his monks, he left unfinished.⁷³ The third is the very long addition, from page 113 to page 165 of the 1689 edition, that recounts the lives and edifying deaths of two monks of La Trappe, one of whom was Dom Jacques Minguet, the former abbot of Châtillon. And the fourth, which is here our immediate concern, is the second part—a sort of Appendix—to the 1689 edition, from page 177 to page 216, which contains the "Historical Account of the Constitutions of the Abbey of Our Lady of La Trappe." What were these Constitutions, what was their authority, and what was their relationship to the 1690 *Règlemens de l'abbaye de Nôtre-Dame de La Trappe en forme de Constitutions*, and the two volumes of the *Règlemens généraux pour l'abbaye de N. D. de La Trappe* published in 1701?

The "Historical Account of the Constitutions of the Abbey of Our Lady of La Trappe" is firmly based on the *Constitutions de l'abbaye de La Trappe*, which was published anonymously at

---

⁷¹ See n. 131 to the translation.
⁷² See n. 108 to the translation.
⁷³ See n. 69 to the translation.

Paris in 1671.[74] Permission to print was given on January 19, 1671, by Gabriel-Nicolas de La Reynie, lieutenant-general of police. There is not the slightest doubt about the source, for Félibien's account, though considerably shorter than the seventy-five pages of the 1671 version, either summarizes the latter or simply quotes it word for word. The *Constitutions de l'abbaye de La Trappe* is a slim duodecimo volume in which the Constitutions themselves are preceded by a laudatory "Discourse on the Reform of the Abbey of La Trappe," of which a complete translation appears as an appendix to this book. It has nothing but praise for Rancé and his reform. Who, then, was responsible for the 1671 *Constitutions*, and what was their authority?

The book has been attributed to Nicolas-Pierre-Henri Montfaucon de Villars (1635–1673),[75] but this attribution has been disputed and seems to me to be most unlikely. Montfaucon de Villars was born to a noble family and educated at the university of Toulouse. Here he showed a distinct predilection for the teachings of the Jewish Talmud and the writings of Plotinus, but he left Toulouse for Paris after a series of misadventures of which the details are lacking. Once in Paris, he spent much of his time in the company of sceptics and freethinkers, and from January to September 1661 found himself imprisoned in the Bastille, though once again the details are unclear. On his release he enjoyed the life of a worldly abbé-about-town, or enjoyed it at least as far as his impecunious circumstances would allow.

What money he made, he made from writing, and his most celebrated work was *Le Comte de Gabalis, ou Entretiens sur les sciences secrètes* ("The Count of Gabalis, or Conversations on

---

[74] *Constitutions de l'abbaye de La Trappe* (Paris: Michel Le Petit & Estienne Michallet, 1671); Tournoüer, no. 360. See also Tournoüer, nos. 361–63, 319–20.

[75] See *DLF XVII*, 1255–56 (with bibliography).

the Secret Sciences"), first published in 1670 and reissued a number of times thereafter. An English translation appeared in 1680. The "Count of Gabalis" is the "Count of the Cabala," and the book consists of five discourses on occult, Rosicrucian, and cabalistic themes. It is a very curious text that deals with elementals, sylphs, undines, gnomes, salamanders, oracles, and marriages between humans and non-humans, and it enjoyed a remarkable success. In 1673, three years after the publication of the work, its author found it expedient to leave Paris—he was a man with a natural ability to get into trouble—and departed for Lyon. He did not arrive, being assassinated on the way in mysterious circumstances. In other writings, he displays a violent antagonism to Jansenism and anything that smelled of Jansenism, and he delivered a series of acerbic attacks on Pascal's *Pensées* and the Solitaries of Port-Royal.[76] It is difficult, I think, to imagine a man of this character, worldly and freethinking, with a deep interest in the Talmud, Plotinus, and the Cabala, setting forth the so-called Constitutions of La Trappe in a sympathetic and positive light, for although Rancé was not, in fact, a Jansenist, he was certainly suspected of being so, and he certainly had Jansenist sympathies.[77] Nor is there any trace of Montfaucon de Villars's ever visiting La Trappe, or, indeed, of ever showing the slightest interest in so doing.

But if Montfaucon de Villars did not compile the *Constitutions*, who did? It was assuredly not Rancé, for he himself was most annoyed by the appearance of the book and more than once denied having anything whatever to do with it. It was printed, as we have said, on January 19, 1671, and towards the end of that year, on December 12, Rancé wrote to Dom Robert or Robin Couturier and included in the letter his own account

---

[76] See his *Traité de la délicatesse*, first published in 1671.
[77] See Krailsheimer, *Rancé*, 259–61, 282–83, and Chap. 15, "Rancé and the Jansenists," 319–28. See also Bell, *Rancé*, 37–39, 136–38.

of the matter. Dom Robert was a friend of Rancé who had been professed at Barbeaux, appointed prior of Preuilly by the reformed General Chapter of 1664, and was prior of Perseigne from 1678 to 1681. Alban Krailsheimer has suggested that in 1671 he was back at Barbeaux, perhaps as cellarer,[78] and that is very probably correct. Rancé's letter to him deals with a number of matters, but the essential part for our purposes reads as follows:

> I will say nothing to you of the history of these supposed *Constitutions* of La Trappe. We see nothing of these sorts of things in our monastery. From what I have been told of them, it seems that they comprise a few small regulations for interior use in the house to which someone has wished to give the name "Constitutions," which they do not deserve. They may contain some things that are not found in the *Usages* since they did not cover everything, though I do not think there is anything that conflicts with their spirit. The principal practices of our monastery are not set forth there. We took everything we could from the *Usages*, but since we may easily have made an error, we have no choice but to give [our] opinions on this, and will happily receive any [opinions] from others.[79]

Rancé's statement that the so-called Constitutions comprise no more than a "few small regulations" (*quelques petits règlements*) may perhaps be taken with a pinch of salt, but there is no doubt that they are based on the Cistercian *Us* or Usages, which, in turn, are to be found in the twelfth-century *Ecclesiastica officia*. There are times when Rancé's regulations go beyond the Usages and even contradict them (as they also occasionally contradict the Rule of Saint Benedict itself), but

---

[78] Rancé, *Correspondance*, 1:417.
[79] Rancé, *Correspondance*, 1:416–17 (Letter 711212).

in the version of the *Règlements* that appeared in 1690, Rancé regularly refers to the *Us* to provide authority for its own regulations.

Nevertheless, he uses the same expression—*quelques petits règlements*—in a letter written three or four months later to an unnamed friend, but in this letter there is not one but two books in circulation that are causing Rancé some annoyance:

> I am infinitely obliged to you for the interest you have the goodness to take in that which concerns us. You judge the two books that are circulating in the world, and that describe what goes on in this house, fairly when you have believed that we had no part in them and that they appeared without our participation. We have a few small regulations setting out the details of our life in this monastery, but they are so inconsequential that they cannot be called "Constitutions." They are very different from those that we have sent to you, though they do agree on some points.[80]

What is the second of the *deux écritures*? It is nothing less than Félibien's *Description de l'abbaye de La Trappe*, and Rancé is adamant that he had nothing to do with either. What he sent to the unnamed friend we do not know, but he does seem to admit, somewhat reluctantly, that there is at least some agreement between the "Constitutions" (Rancé clearly objects to the word) and what actually went on at the abbey. "On some points" (*en quelques articles*) must, I suspect, be treated like "a few small regulations." A comparison of the "Constitutions" and the 1690 *Règlements*, which certainly came from Rancé's pen, shows agreement on a very great number of points.

There is then a silence for some seven years, and the next we hear of the "Constitutions" (or, as here, "Statutes") is in two

---

[80] Rancé, *Correspondance*, 1:421 (Letter 72/3).

letters to Rancé's old tutor, Jean Favier.[81] In both he strongly denies that he had anything to do with them, and in the second letter he mentions the *Refléxions* on the "Constitutions," which were also published for the first time in 1671.[82] The first letter dates from December 3, 1689: "I do not know what is meant by the "Statutes" of La Trappe. It did not occur to me to have what we do among ourselves printed, since we live, so far as we are able, as did our Fathers, and we try to imitate and follow them."[83] The second was written a year and a half later, on May 25, 1681: "I will say no more about these supposed *Constitutions of La Trappe*. I know that they have been printed under this title, and that there have even been added to them certain *Reflections*; but the truth, as I have already written to you, is that I had no part whatever in this. One can attribute to me whatever one likes, but that does not make me responsible."[84]

But if neither Montaucon de Villars nor Rancé published the "Constitutions," who did? Rancé's own account of what happened appears in a most important letter to the abbé Jacques Tétu, an old friend of Rancé (they were the same age) who enjoyed the favor of the royal court and was a royal preacher, a *prédicateur du roi*. The letter was written on October 26, 1690, almost twenty years after the 1671 publication of the *Constitutions* and just about two months after the publication of the 1690 *Règlements*. This is Rancé's brief account: "As far as the *Règlements* are concerned, Monsieur, you must know that they are given to the novices during their novitiate, and they may make copies of them without our knowing. Often, they have even taken away the originals with them, and these

---

[81] See n. 43 above.

[82] *Réflexions sur les Constitutions de l'abbaye de La Trappe* (Paris: Claude Barbin, 1671; Paris: Louis Billaine, 1671; Villefranche: Pierre Grandsaigne, 1671).

[83] Rancé, *Correspondance*, 2:324 (Letter 791203a).

[84] Rancé, *Correspondance*, 2:520 (Letter 810525).

are the very ones that were printed twenty years ago and on which a prelate made certain *Reflections* which were also printed."⁸⁵ So according to Rancé, it was a novice or novices from La Trappe who leaked the regulations, and a certain prelate who composed the *Réflexions*. A prelate—*prélat*—refers to a high-ranking ecclesiastic, usually but not necessarily a bishop, and that (as we shall see) is important. The account that appears in the pages of Louis Dubois's *Histoire de l'abbé de Rancé*, however, is slightly different. "The manuscript regulations of La Trappe," he tells us, "fell into the hands of someone who had come there to make a retreat. He took them away secretly to Paris and gave them to a printer to be published, hoping, by means of their publication, to reveal to the world a true account of life in this holy desert and do away with the misunderstandings. The work appeared in two parts, the first under the title *Constitutions of the Abbey of La Trappe*, and the second as *Reflections on the said Constitutions*."⁸⁶ The novice or novices have now become someone who made a retreat at the abbey, and Dubois implies that this person, presumably Rancé's "prelate," was responsible for both the *Constitutions* and the *Reflections*. Can we take the matter any further? Perhaps we can.

When the *Reflections* were printed from 1671 onwards, a small number of the editions attributed the work to a certain "abbé de Lignage," and it has been suggested (as, for example, in the catalogue of the *Bibliothèque nationale de France*) that the "abbé de Lignage" (who is otherwise unknown) was a pseudonym for none other than our cabalistic adventurer, Nicolas-Pierre-Henri Montfaucon de Villars. This, as I have suggested, is infinitely unlikely. It may, however, contain a grain of truth, for there was another "abbé de Villars" who is a far more likely candidate. Of whom are we speaking here?

⁸⁵ Rancé, *Correspondance*, 4:57–58 (Letter 901026).
⁸⁶ Dubois, *Rancé*, 1:393.

He was Henri-Félix de Villars, commendatory abbot of the abbey of Montier (or Monstier, Moutier, Monthiers)-en-Argonne, in the diocese of Châlons-sur-Marne, and a man whom Rancé knew. He was the son of Pierre de Villars—the marquis de Villars (1623–1698)—and therefore the scion of a most distinguished family. His elder brother was Claude-Louis-Hector de Villars, perhaps the most brilliant of Louis XIV's commanders and one of only six marshals ever to be promoted to the exalted rank of Marshal-General of France. Furthermore, their father, Pierre de Villars, married Marie Gigault de Bellefonds, the aunt of Bernardin Gigault, marshal de Bellefonds, who, in turn, was one of Rancé's closest friends and a regular correspondent.[87]

On April 23, 1682, and again on November 25, 1685, Rancé wrote to the marshal de Bellefonds saying that the abbot of Clairvaux (Pierre IV Bouchu at the time) was doing what he could to establish good order in the abbey of Montier, but that there was a slight difficulty with regard to the building of a certain enclosing wall (the details need not concern us).[88] "Monsieur the abbé de Villars, your nephew" (Rancé gets the family relationship wrong) is not happy about this, and Rancé asks the marshal to persuade Henri-Félix to accede to the abbot of Clairvaux's request for the wall to be built. "At its root," says Rancé, "the position of a commendatory abbot has nothing to justify it before God, nor to give it legitimacy, save the diligence with which he works to see that [God] is served and honored in his house, and the devotion with which he acquits himself in the duties to which he is bound by his original institution."[89] It is clear, however, that unlike most commendatory abbots, Henri-Félix de Villars took an active interest in the running of

---

[87] See Rancé, *Correspondance*, 4:585–86.

[88] Rancé, *Correspondance*, 2:636–39 (Letter 820423) and 3:315–17 (Letter 851125).

[89] Rancé, *Correspondance*, 2:638–39 (Letter 820423).

his monastery. He might have done more had he not died young in October 1691 at Florence, on his way back to France from a journey to Rome.[90]

There is no evidence, so far as I know, that Henri-Félix ever made a retreat at La Trappe, but as a commendatory abbot of a celebrated family and noble lineage,[91] he would certainly deserve to be referred to as a "prelate." I think it quite possible, therefore, if not probable, that it was he who was responsible for the compilation and publication of the *Constitutions* and *Réflexions* that caused Rancé such annoyance. It is even possible that he received a manuscript copy of the *Constitutions* from a novice of La Trappe, and that the accounts of what happened by Rancé and, later, Louis Dubois are not entirely contradictory. The *Constitutions* were published with the best of intentions, and "The Discourse on the Reform of the Abbey of La Trappe" that precedes them has, as we have mentioned, nothing but good to say of Rancé's work at the abbey and his devotion in bringing back the first spirit of the Rule of Saint Benedict. Nor is it difficult to explain how Henri-Félix de Villars came to be confused with the author of *Le Comte de Gabalis*. The latter book had been published in 1670, the year before the *Constitutions* and *Réflexions*, and had proved remarkably popular. Anyone in 1671, therefore, hearing the name "the abbé de Villars" would naturally think of the well-known Nicolas-Pierre-Henri Montfaucon de Villars and not the commendatory abbot of Montier-en-Argonne. In other words, the "abbé de Lignage," who appears on the title page of a number

---

[90] See *Gallia Christiana* IX (1751): 970, and Pierre Bayle, *Dictionnaire historique et critique de Pierre Bayle. Nouvelle édition* (Paris: P. Desoer, 1820), 14:398. The *Gallia Christiana* incorrectly has the abbot dying in Rome.

[91] The "Lignage" of the "abbé de Lignage" may actually mean "lineage," as in (for example) *une demoiselle de haut lignage*, "a maiden of high degree."

of editions of the *Réflexions*, was indeed very probably the "abbé de Villars," but there were two "abbés de Villars," and the general public, understandably, got the wrong one.

The publication of the so-called *Constitutions* placed Rancé in something of a quandary. Was he to do anything about them? It is clear that they were, in fact, a fairly accurate account of life at La Trappe—they were more than "a few small regulations"—but they could not be called, in any official sense, "Constitutions," "Statutes," or "Regulations." As Alban Krailsheimer has said, what Rancé was denying in the letters we have translated above "is not so much the facts disclosed in these documents as their official status."[92] That the novices at the abbey must have had some guide to the reformed monastic life is obvious, and it is equally obvious that such a guide was compiled from documents that had been produced as and when needed. In the 1690 *Règlemens*, for example, the infirmarian is instructed to place a copy of the regulations relating to the sick in the infirmary into the hands of each new patient,[93] and as Martinus Cawley has pointed out, chapters fifteen and sixteen of the *Règlemens* "present themselves as long-existing written texts, destined for the attention of the guest-house staff."[94] Chapter fourteen, "Some Rules and General Practices," looks very much like an early provisional list of regulations that has been appended to the complete collection, and some of the material that appears there could more appropriately be included in other chapters.

By 1690 Rancé had decided to publish (anonymously) an official and considerably expanded version of the "Constitutions" under the title *Règlemens de l'abbaye de Nôtre-Dame de*

---

[92] Krailsheimer, *Rancé*, 87.

[93] See *Règlemens*, 87 (XII.12).

[94] *The Regulations of the Abbey of La Trappe in the Form of Constitutions*, trans. John Baptist Hasbrouck, intro. by Martinus Cawley (Lafayette: Guadalupe Translations, 1999), xi, and see x–xiii generally.

La Trappe en forme de Constitutions.[95] The title is significant, for it implies that these *Constitutions* may truly be called "Constitutions" and that they wholly supersede the unauthorized and unofficial so-called Constitutions of 1671. In both collections, however, the various sections follow precisely the same order. Both begin with the regulations for the church, and then proceed with those for the Dormitory, Refectory, Warming Room, Cloisters, Manual Labor, Conference, Chapter of Faults, and Infirmary. Both end with the chapter containing the General Rules and Practices. The 1690 *Règlemens* adds more material in all the sections and has additional chapters on participation in the sacraments, outdoor walks, bloodletting, and regulations for guests, but the relationship between the two is clear and obvious. Sometimes the 1690 Regulations contradict the 1670 Constitutions—whether the monks may read in their cells is a good example[96]—but this is not common. Further regulations and further commentary were added following the publication of the 1690 volume, and the final *Règlemens généraux pour l'abbaye de N. D. de La Trappe* appeared, this time under the author's name, in two volumes in 1701.[97] By this time, the regulations have expanded to almost 750 pages, but the 1701 volumes must be regarded in the same light as the Mishnah, the authoritative code of Jewish law compiled by Rabbi Judah the Prince between 180 and 220 C.E. Both are spiritual treatises in their own rights, and far more than merely long lists of rules and regulations. By 1701, however, both Rancé and Félibien were dead, and a study of the 1701 regulations is not here our concern.

---

[95] See Tournoüer, nos. 364–68. A manuscript copy and numerous printed editions were to be found in the library of La Trappe: see Bell, *Library*, 538 (R.31–32).
[96] See n. 92 to the translation.
[97] Tournoüer, no. 366, published at Paris by François Muguet.

To return, then, to the "Historical Account of the Constitutions of the Abbey of Our Lady of La Trappe," which comprises the second part of the 1689 edition of Félibien's *Description*. What can we say of them after this long digression? I would suggest that we can say three things. First, they are unquestionably based on the *Constitutions* published anonymously in January 1671, and the author of these *Constitutions* was most probably Henri-Félix de Villars, commendatory abbot of Montier-en-Argonne. It was not Nicolas-Pierre-Henri Montfaucon de Villars. Second, although Rancé had nothing to do with their publication and rejected the description of them as "Constitutions," there is every reason to believe that they are an accurate reflection of the regulations in use at La Trappe in Rancé's early years as abbot of the reformed monastery. And third, when we take Félibien's *Description* together with the abbreviated version of the *Constitutions* that appear in the 1689 edition of that book, what we have is as faithful and as reliable a picture as we can hope to get of life at La Trappe under the Great Reformer. It is true that we have to see it through a somewhat rose-colored and adulatory mist, but enough good, solid fact remains to provide us with a fascinating tour through an abbey that itself was a source of fascination to a very great number of people in seventeenth-century France.

Description of the Abbey of La Trappe

The Bookseller to the Reader[1]

The great things that are happening in our days can sometimes become so familiar to us by round-the-clock reporting that it seems useless to write of them unless it be for the instruction of those who will come after us. And very often we think we know as much about them as those who are involved in publicizing them. This is not the case with the abbey of La Trappe. A great to-do is made about the way of life of Monsieur l'Abbé[2] and the monks who have withdrawn there. They are discussed, they are admired, but whatever is said of them, everyone wants to see [the abbey] for themselves so as to gain an idea that measures up to the truth. Some, amazed at what they have heard of this house, have gone there themselves to ascertain the facts of what seems to them by nature impossible. Others have flocked there being convinced that merely by seeing these models of virtue they themselves would be moved to true repentance and would take on [a life of] penance and penitence[3] with no difficulty. Yet others, so deeply affected by the humility of Monsieur l'Abbé [de Rancé], his zeal for God, and his vigilant care for the way of life of his monks, have

---

[1] This introduction, *Le Libraire au Lecteur*, does not appear in the first (1671) edition of the *Description*. In the new edition of 1689, it is followed by the *Extrait du Privilège du Roy*, which, in the 1671 edition, appears in a different form at the end.

[2] In the *Description*, "Monsieur l'Abbé" is always Monsieur l'Abbé de Rancé.

[3] *Pénitence*, in French, can mean penitence, penance, or repentance, or any combination of all three.

sought to speak with him so that, through that nourishment, they might continue to live the holy life they have led up to then. All have returned so full of what they have seen that they cannot refrain from broadcasting it, not only to their friends, but to anyone else of their acquaintance.

Yet far from satisfying people's curiosity, these widespread accounts, coming from all directions, have given rise to a great desire to know every detail [of life at La Trappe], and persons of quality have shown greater eagerness in this matter than any others. Witness the example of the Illustrious Lady[4] to whom this description is addressed: she gave the author no peace until he took pen in hand. And so, as a result of her continual pleading, he had no choice but to write down what he had seen at La Trappe all those times he had been there and to add to that a history of the Order, which he had studied from its foundation. It is this that leads us to say that[5] *the Author of this Description shows us that true examples of humility can be found in the world as well as at La Trappe, for with true self-sacrifice he has obeyed the instructions he received by allowing his work to be printed, a work which is no less useful than it is a pleasure to read.*

---

[4] I.e., Jeanne de Schomberg, duchess of Liancourt (1600–1674), who is discussed in the Introduction to this translation.

[5] The italicized section that follows appears in italics in the original.

Description of the Abbey of La Trappe (1689)
To Madame The Duchess Of Liancourt[1]

Madame,

It is not without reason that I fear I have not wholly satisfied your devout curiosity, for I find great difficulty in providing you with a description of the abbey of La Trappe that could correspond to the high idea one should have of it. Nevertheless, so far as I am able, I shall do my best to satisfy you and provide you on this occasion with a few proofs of my obedience, and I shall tell you exactly all that I have.

I will therefore say to you that on the last journey I made there,[2] I took particular care not only to take note of its situation and to observe the way of life of these latter-day anchorites, but also, by addressing myself to those persons who have a perfect knowledge of the matter, to inform myself as best I could of [the details of] the foundation of the house and of all that has happened there up till now. And not being content with that, Madame, you will see that while I was staying at the abbey and during the time that the monks were at work, I even drew up a plan of the whole of their monastery.[3] This I am sending to you so as to give you an idea of how their house

---

[1] Jeanne de Schomberg, duchess of Liancourt (1600–1674): see the Introduction to this translation.

[2] Between September and Christmas 1670: see Krailsheimer, *Rancé*, 86.

[3] The plan, with east at the top, appears at the very beginning of the 1689 edition of the *Description*: see **Figure 1**, p. 26.

is set out, just as I intend to give you [an account of] their way of life.

This abbey is situated in a broad valley, and the forest and hills surrounding it are arranged in such a way that it seems that they wish to hide it from the rest of the earth. They enclose the cultivable areas, the plantations of fruit trees, the pastures, and nine ponds that lie around the abbey and that make the approach to it so difficult that it is not easy to reach even with the help of a guide.[4] In the past, there was a road going from

---

[4] Do not be deceived by the ease with which one can get to the abbey today. La Trappe lies on the very edge of the Forêt Domaniale du Perche et de La Trappe, a little to the northwest of the village of Soligny-la-Trappe, and the D251 road runs right in front of its main gate. The railway station of L'Aigle is just 18 kms away. All these roads, however, are from the nineteenth century, and access to the abbey before then was a hazardous experience. When William Dorset Fellowes visited La Trappe in 1817, he needed a guide (only one could be found who knew the way), and he went "armed with pistols and a sword-cane, in case of meeting with wolves," which, he had been informed, abounded in the region. They traveled through a countryside that appeared scarcely inhabited, through a thick and almost impenetrable forest (where they were alarmed by the howl of a wolf), and then over a rocky plain where there were a few flocks of sheep and goats. They then entered the forest of Bellegarde, which is "so dark and intricate, that those best acquainted with it frequently lose their way." There were no traces of human footsteps, no animal tracks, and when they finally escaped from the gloom of the trees they found themselves on the brow of a precipitous hill that they descended by way of a winding labyrinthine path that led them down to the bottom of a valley. There, surrounded by its lakes, was "the venerable abbey of La Trappe, with its dark gray towers, the deep tone of whose bell had previously announced to us, that we had nearly reached our journey's end" (William D. Fellowes, *A Visit to the Monastery of La Trappe in 1817: with Notes Taken During a Tour Through Le Perche, Normandy, Bretagne, Poitou, Anjou, Le Bocage, Tourraine, Orleanois, and the Environs of Paris* [London: W. Stockdale, 1818], 5–8).

Mortagne to Paris[5] that passed behind the walls of the garden, but even though it was in the woods and more than five hundred paces from the monastic enclosure, and even though it could not be moved further away without great expense, Monsieur l'Abbé [de Rancé][6] nevertheless had it changed so that the area around their monastery would be less frequented. There is therefore nothing more solitary than this desert, for even though there may be a number of towns and villages at three leagues[7] round about, it nevertheless seems that one is in a strange country and a foreign land. Everywhere silence reigns. If you hear any sound at all, it is only the sound of trees blowing in the wind and streams flowing over stones.

You see the abbey when you come out of the Forest of the Perche from the south, but although it now looks very close, you have to go nearly another league before you actually reach it. But finally, having come down the mountain, crossed the heath, and walked for some time through groves of [oak]-trees[8] on shady paths, you arrive at the First Courtyard and the lodging of the Guest Master.[9] This [court] is separated from that of

---

[5] Mortagne-au-Perche is 11 kms south of La Trappe and 162 kms west of Paris. Paris and Mortagne are now joined by the N12 highway; the old road lay a little to the north of the modern N12. William Fellowes lists its various stages and tells us that the roads were excellent and the countryside beautiful (Fellowes, *Visit*, 2).

[6] In the *Description*, Monsieur l'Abbé is always Armand-Jean de Rancé. His abbacy and his friendship with André Félibien are discussed in the Introduction to this translation.

[7] Probably about 10 kms. The old French league of 10,000 *pieds* ("feet") or 3.248 kms was standard in many, but not all, parts of France until 1674. It was then redefined as exactly 2000 *toises* ("fathoms") or just about 3.898 kms.

[8] We know they were oaks from Fellowes's description (*Visit*, 10). They were all cut down at the Revolution.

[9] This is the Courtyard at the southwest corner of the enclosure. The Guest Master's lodging is Building no. 2 in the Plan (**figure 1**). Building no. 1 at the northeast corner of the Courtyard is the Gate Chapel.

the monks by a stout palisade of wooden stakes and thorny bushes that Monsieur l'Abbé had made when he withdrew [from the world]. Here, you ring the bell at the gate and a lay brother comes to open it.[10] You [then] enter another large court, very spacious and planted with fruit trees, on the right of which is a dovecote[11] and on the left another lower court where one finds the granaries, storerooms, stables, cowsheds, and other places necessary for the convent's everyday needs.[12] Adjoining this lower courtyard is a mill.[13] It is turned by water

---

[10] We are now at Building no. 3 on the Plan—the Porter's Lodging—situated in the centre of the wooden palisade.

[11] Building no. 4 on **Figure 1**. Dovecotes were a standard feature of medieval and early modern monasteries and provided three extremely useful commodities: meat (like dark chicken meat and very tasty), an excellent fertilizer sometimes referred to as *colombine*, and feathers that could be used for stuffing pillows, cushions, and the like. The birds could also be sold. Pigeon or dove eggs, though small, are also perfectly edible. Cistercians of the Strict Observance were rigorously vegetarian—a conflict over meat eating was the main reason for their coming into existence—and feather pillows formed no part of life at La Trappe. Nor did the monks market the birds. But fertilizer was essential for a community striving to be self-sufficient. Meat might be served in the infirmary, but (as we shall see in due course) not the meat of pigeons or doves.

[12] This is the *Basse Court du Convent* on **Figure 1**: the stables for the horses are Building no. 6; the cowsheds are Building no. 7.

[13] This is the *moulin* to the south of Buildings no. 6 and no. 7. The mill race is now sealed off, but a mill was operating here in the nineteenth century. The building adjoining it, marked *Cave Four et Grenier* (cellar, oven, and attic/storeroom), still survives and is the only medieval structure remaining from the ancient abbey. It is an impressive building with two stories and an attic, of which a description and illustrations of the interior and exterior may be found in Terryl N. Kinder, *Cistercian Europe. Architecture of Contemplation* (Grand Rapids, Cambridge, Kalamazoo: W. B. Eerdmans, 2002), 372–73, Plates 14 IVb, IVc, and V. Dr Kinder suggests an industrial origin for the building (373).

from a stream that flows from the ponds and that, after separating the Great Courtyard from the Monks' Garden beside the church, runs under another part of the same courtyard before making its way into a reservoir.[14] But before speaking to you of the monastery and the monks who dwell there today, I believe, Madame, that it would be appropriate to tell you something of the foundation of this house, how it achieved its reform, and, after that, [to describe] the great austerity that characterizes it at present.

The Abbey of Our Lady of the House of God of La Trappe—for such is its name—was founded by Rotrou, count of the Perche, in 1140[15] and consecrated in the name of the Holy Virgin in 1214 by Robert, archbishop of Rouen; Raoul, bishop of Evreux; and Sylvester, bishop of Séez.[16] For a very long time

---

[14] This is the *ruisseau* "stream" shown on the right (south) of **Figure 1**, just above the dovecote. The *jardin* "garden" lies beyond the east end of the church. The stream disappears underground just below Building no. 32 and then resurfaces to flow into the reservoir (no. 5), which fed the mill race.

[15] As we saw in the Introduction, the early history of the abbey is actually a little more complicated. The memorial chapel erected by Rotrou III was probably consecrated in 1122, and sometime after 1137—the precise date is unknown—Rotrou invited six monks from the Savigniac abbey of Breuil-Benoît, situated not far from the Perche in the valley of the Eure, to come to the site and transform it into a proper religious house. Then, on December 2, 1140, Rotrou made a formal donation of a substantial amount of land to La Trappe, and it is the date of this donation that is usually cited (as Félibien cites it) as the date of the foundation of the new abbey. The 1140 donation was less generous than it appears: the land was some of the worst in the Perche.

[16] From 1189 to 1243—more than fifty years—the abbot of La Trappe was Adam Gauthier, a devout and eminently able man who was also a great builder. During his abbacy the monastery was considerably enlarged and a new or rebuilt church was consecrated on April 27, 1214, by Robert III Poulain (also called Robert le Baube), archbishop of Rouen from1208 to 1221, assisted by the bishops of Evreux and

it experienced the effects of the decadence of the Order of Cîteaux, and fell into that dissolute state that, as everyone knows, can still be seen in many monasteries of the Order that have been living in laxity for the last two hundred years, [monasteries] that never embraced the strict observance of the Rule [of Saint Benedict] reestablished in France by the late Cardinal de La Rochefoucauld.[17] It was [forty years] after this that Messire Armand-Jean [Le] Bouthillier de Rancé,[18] Doctor of Theology,[19] chief almoner of the late Monsieur the Duke of Orleans,[20] and commendatory abbot of this abbey for more

---

Séez. Félibien is correct in referring to Sylvester of Séez, bishop from 1202 to 1220, but wrong in referring to Raoul of Evreux. The bishop in 1214 was Lucas of Evreux, who administered the see from 1203 to 1220. Raoul I de Cierrey was his successor (bishop from 1220 to 1223).

[17] In 1622 Cardinal François de La Rochefoucauld (1558–1645) had been appointed by Pope Gregory XV as Apostolic Visitor to oversee the reform of the old religious orders in France, a reform that was certainly necessary and that was not confined to the Cistercians. By this time, the Abstinent movement had a strong following in the Cistercian Order, having been established by Octave Arnolfini, abbot of La Charmoye, in 1603. La Rochefoucauld, a devout ascetic with a fervent desire for reform, immediately gave his wholehearted support to the Abstinents. This was the first phase of what has been called the War of the Observances. For a brief account, see Bell, *Rancé*, 60–62, and for a much more comprehensive discussion, Lekai, *Rise*, 39–61. In 1622 Rancé was not even a thought in his parents' minds—he was born in 1626—and the reform of La Trappe lay far in the future.

[18] After his entry into La Trappe, Rancé ceased to use the family name Bouthillier (or Le Bouthillier). See Bell, *Rancé*, xvi n. 2.

[19] Rancé received his doctorate in theology in February 1654: see Dubois, *Rancé*, 1:66–67.

[20] An almoner was originally an ecclesiastic whose main duty was the distribution of alms to the poor, but by the seventeenth century the almoner to a lord—in this case the duke of Orléans—might also act as a chaplain or advisor in religious matters and (in modern terms) as the person in charge of Public Relations. It must be admitted, however, that the position was something of a sinecure. "The late

than twenty-five years,[21] by his care and frequent exhortations, persuaded the monks of the abbey to agree to and, [indeed,]

Monsieur the Duke of Orleans" was Gaston Jean-Baptiste de France (1608–1660), the third son of Henry IV of France and his wife Marie de Medici; Henry had received the title of duke of Orléans in 1626. He was the oldest surviving brother of the king, Louis XIII, and, according to tradition, was known at court simply as "Monsieur." Rancé's appointment as chief almoner in June 1656 was because of his uncle, Victor Bouthillier, archbishop of Tours from 1641 to his death in 1670, who had occupied the position previously. The archbishop, as Louis Dubois puts it, "songeait toujours a l'avenir de son neveu" (Dubois, *Rancé*, 1:88). The duke died on February 2, 1660. For a detailed account of the matter, see Dubois, *Rancé*, 1:88–92.

[21] The system of commendatory superiors—religious houses held *in commendam* or "in trust"—had its origins in the desire of the popes of the Avignon papacy (1309–1376) to keep tighter control over ecclesiastical benefices. Abbots would no longer be elected by their own communities, but appointed by the pope or local ruler. The abbots so appointed were normally secular prelates who were given the abbeys as a reward for services rendered, and, for the most part, they were no more than absentee landlords whose main concern was to pocket as much of the monastic revenues as they could. With but a few exceptions, the commendatory system was an unmitigated disaster for French monasticism. See further Bell, *Rancé*, 53–55. Rancé's elder brother, Denis, had been intended for the church and was commendatory superior of five houses, but on his untimely (though not unexpected) death in 1637, his future prospects and his benefices passed to his younger brother. Thus, in that year, the eleven-year-old Armand-Jean found himself reaping the revenues of the Benedictine abbey of Saint-Symphorien in Beauvais, the Benedictine priory of Saint-Clémentin near Poitiers, the Grandmontine priory of Boulogne near Chambord, the Augustinian abbey of Notre-Dame-du-Val situated between Falaise and Caen, and the dilapidated Cistercian abbey of La Trappe in the wild wastes of Normandy (Dubois, *Rancé*, 1:19–20). The total income from the five houses seems to have been substantial—about 16,000 *livres per annum* (Dubois, *Rancé*, 20)—and the Bouthillier family had no intention of losing it.

to make their own request,[22] that [the abbey] be placed in the hands of the Fathers of the Strict Observance of Cîteaux, so as to reestablish [at La Trappe] the first and true observance of the Rule [of Saint Benedict].[23]

The abbot of Barbery of the Strict Observance and Visitor of the Province [of Normandy],[24] came to [the abbey] at the request

---

[22] Félibien is wearing rose-colored spectacles here. By 1660 Rancé had begun to realize that God was indeed calling him to the monastic life, and over the next two years he sold his country estate at Véretz, transferred the benefices he held *in commendam*, contacted the authorities of the Cistercian Strict Observance, and asked them to send to La Trappe five or six religious from the abbey of Perseigne, which had embraced the reform more than twenty years earlier (see n. 31 below). Rancé's attempts at reform were met with determined resistance and violent hostility from the six monks and one lay brother who were living at La Trappe in what Alban Krailsheimer has called "undisciplined squalor" (Krailsheimer, *Legacy*, 24), and his "frequent exhortations" had no effect whatever. Eventually, realizing that his endeavors were useless, he had no choice but to establish the legal agreement (*concordat*) with the recalcitrant religious mentioned in n. 26 below.

[23] During his difficult novitiate at Perseigne (June 1663–June 1664) Rancé had been profoundly affected by a book written by Julien Paris, abbot of Foucarmont: *Du premier esprit de l'ordre de Cîteaux*, first published in 1653. What was the *premier esprit* of the Order? Nothing less than that strict and unswerving fidelity to the Rule of Saint Benedict that Rancé demanded at La Trappe. See further, Bell, *Understanding Rancé*, 128–33.

[24] Nicolas III Le Guédois, abbot of Barbery (19 kms from Caen) from 1651 (when Louis II Quinet resigned the abbacy) until his death in 1677. He was appointed Visitor for the Province of Normandy in 1660 and 1664. See *Gallia Christiana* XIV:455–56 (which gives his epitaph) and (with correct dates) Honoré Fisquet, *La France pontificale (Gallia Christiana). Histoire chronologique et biographique des Archevêques et Évêques de tous les Diocèses de France. Métropole de Rouen. Bayeux et Lisieux* (Paris: E. Repos, 1866), 210. The abbey of Notre-Dame de Barbery had a reputation for asceticism equaling that of La Trappe under Rancé.

of Monsieur l'Abbé de Rancé with a commission from the abbot of Prières, the vicar general,[25] and established a legal agreement between Monsieur l'Abbé and the former monks of La Trappe on August 17, 1662. This was then ratified by the Parliament of Paris on February 16, 1663.[26] By virtue of this, the monks of the Strict Observance would enter the monastery and take possession of it, and in order to provide them with a better means of establishing themselves there, Monsieur l'Abbé donated to them the Terre de Nuisement,[27] whose [possession] he had enjoyed as commendatory abbot.

When they began the work of reestablishing the monastery and trying to revive there the first spirit[28] of the fathers and saints who were its founders, Monsieur l'Abbé, who, for a number of years, had retired from the world and had divested himself of numerous abbeys and other benefices he possessed[29] in order to think solely of his salvation, was inspired by God to embrace in his abbey of La Trappe the life of the Strict Observance; having conceived such an ardent desire, he obtained

---

[25] Jean VI Jouaud, abbot of Prières in Brittany for forty-two years, from 1631 to 1673 (*Gallia Christiana* XIV:967). He played a fundamental role in the reform movement and the establishment of the Strict Observance. See further Lekai, *Rise*, 53–151.

[26] See n. 22 above. The *concordat* provided each of the former religious with a pension of four hundred *livres* and gave them permission either to remain at La Trappe or to retire to some other monastery (Dubois, *Rancé*, 1:221–22). Only one monk remained; all the others left. The one who remained was Joseph Bernier, and Félibien tells the story of his life and (especially) his exemplary death in the pages below (see n. 135 foll.).

[27] Situated at Sainte-Colombe-sur-Risle, a short distance northeast of L'Aigle (which is 18 kms from La Trappe and the nearest railway station to the abbey). See Léopold V. Delisle, *Études sur la condition de la class agricole et l'état de l'agriculture en Normandie, au Moyen Âge* (Evreux: A. Hérissey, 1851), 91.

[28] *Le premier esprit*: see n. 23 above.

[29] See n. 21 above.

from the king permission to hold this abbey as regular [abbot] by a royal warrant granted to him on May 10, 1663.[30] He then took the regular habit and was admitted to the novitiate in the monastery of Our Lady of Perseigne, of the Strict Observance of Cîteaux,[31] on June 13, being at that time thirty-seven years and five months old.

On March 12, 1664, while Rancé was still commendatory abbot, even though he had taken the religious habit, he went from Perseigne to La Trappe. There, in the chapter room and in the presence of the whole community, he read aloud a will he had made in favor of the Fathers of the Strict Observance of this house, and confirmed by word of mouth the intentions he had expressed in this will. In order to carry out the terms [of the document] in their entirety, he dispossessed himself of whatever property he had in the monastery, and especially of all his books.[32] These he put in the hands of the monks, on

---

[30] The king was Louis XIV, and the ground for Rancé's request had been prepared by Jean Jouaud (see n. 25) and Père François Annat, the king's Jesuit confessor from 1654 to 1670, who had the ear of Anne of Austria, the Queen Mother. She, "with her customary wisdom and piety, removed all obstacles" (Dubois, *Rancé*, 1:235). The royal warrant (*brevet*) granted Rancé permission to become regular abbot, but included the provision that if he should die or resign his office, then the abbey would immediately return to being *in commendam* (Dubois, *Rancé*, 1:235).

[31] According to the *Gallia Christiana* XIV:518, the monks of Perseigne had embraced the "stricter observance of the Benedictine Rule" (*strictiorem Benedictinae regulae observantiam*) on July 3, 1637. The abbey itself remained *in commendam*; the priors were responsible for implementing and continuing the reform. The commendatory abbot at this time was Roger de Harlay de Césy (1615–1669), bishop of Lodève from 1657 to his death in 1669: see Fisquet, *La France pontificale. Métropole d'Avignon. Montpellier (2ème partie), contenant Béziers, Lodève, Saint-Pons de Tombières* (Paris: E. Repos, 1855), 460–62.

[32] For a full and detailed account of Rancé's books—where they came from, what they were, their number, and what happened to them—see Bell, *Library*, especially chaps. 2 and 3 (pp. 17–48).

condition that they not be taken out of the abbey, nor placed anywhere else for any reason whatever. His intention was that they would serve for the use and instruction of the reformed religious of the house. And if, through unforeseen circumstances, the abbey should return into the hands of the former monks and the reform cease to be, his library was to be given to the Hôtel Dieu in Paris[33] to be sold and the money used to feed the poor and the sick. He went on to state that he made this deposition in favor of the reformed religious of the house and of those who would succeed them in the same Observance. He did not want his successor [as regular abbot] to have any share in it, nor to be able to lay claim to anything, nor even to have any use of the books without the agreement and permission of the monks of the house.

On June 26 following [1664], Rancé received from the Court of Rome the letters [permitting him] to hold the abbey of La Trappe (which he still possessed *in commendam*) as regular abbot, and then made his profession at Perseigne in the presence of Dom Michel Guiton,[34] the representative of the

---

[33] The Hôtel-Dieu stood immediately adjacent to the great cathedral of Notre-Dame and was the oldest hospital in Paris. In the same year that Rancé read his will in the chapter house of La Trappe, the hospital was visited by an English traveler, Edward Browne, who described it as "a brave Hospital indeed, in which there are four hundred sick persons. There are four rows of beds stande in a roome, very handsome ones" (John Lough, *France Observed in the Seventeenth Century by British Travellers* [Stocksfield: Oriel Press, 1985], 84). But at the time Rancé read his will, the hospital was overcrowded and poorly ventilated. The nuns did their best, but the problem lay in numbers. "The Sick" wrote Browne, "are very carefully look'd to by an hundred Nuns, with divers other Servants, who told us that they had at least one thousand eight hundred under their Hands, and that the number sometimes exceeded two thousand" (Lough, *France Observed*, 84).

[34] Michel Guiton (ca. 1628–1689) made his profession at Perseigne on March 3, 1647, and was elected prior of the abbey in 1662. In the absence of the commendatory abbot, Roger de Harlay de Césy (see

Reverend Father Vicar General [Jean Jouaud]. With him were two other novices, one of whom was one of his former servants, who, following his example, had left the world and wished to follow him into the desert.[35] And two days later yet another monk made his profession in the same place for the same abbey.

On the last day of the same month, Messire Pierre Félibien, priest, Bachelor of Theology of the Faculty of Paris, and prior of Saint-Clémentin,[36] took possession of the abbey of La Trappe

---

n. 31 above), he was a staunch supporter of the reform. He was removed from his priorate in somewhat obscure circumstances later in 1664 and ten years after that was appointed by Louis XIV to the abbacy of Saint-Benoît-en-Woëvre in the diocese of Metz. He resigned the abbacy in 1685 and retired to the abbey of Notre-Dame de l'Étoile, not far from Poitiers. See Claude Garda, "L'initiateur de Rancé à la vie cistercienne: Dom Michel Guiton, abbé en Lorraine et prédicateur en Poitou," Cîteaux—Commentarii cistercienses 36 (1985): 178–87.

[35] There seems to be some confusion here. According to Dubois, Rancé, 1:242, 561–62, Rancé's former valet de chambre was Antoine Noël, who became a novice at Perseigne on the same day—June 13, 1663—as his former master. He took the name Brother Anthony (frère Antoine) in honour of Saint Anthony of Padua (Dubois, Rancé, 1:242). He was professed on July 15, 1664, and ended his days on March 5, 1695, at the abbey of Tamié in the Savoie region of France (Dubois, Histoire, 125, no. 8). The two who were professed with Rancé on June 26, 1664, were Robert Prudhomme, aged thirty-five, who died on September 19, 1701, not too long after Rancé, and Brother Louis Marchis, aged twenty-two, who died on March 26, 1678: see Dubois, Rancé, 1:252, 255, and Dubois, Histoire, 124, no. 4; 125, no. 7.

[36] Pierre Félibien was a friend of Rancé and an occasional correspondent. He is sometimes said to have been the brother of André Félibien des Avaux, the author of the Description, but that is not the case. The Benedictine priory of Saint-Clémentin near Poitiers had been held in commendam by Rancé (see n. 21 above), and when he dispossessed himself of his benefices, he gave Saint-Clémentin to Félibien. Félibien accompanied Rancé on the Roman mission (see n. 49 below) and wrote an account of his experiences that, alas, has been lost. He died on April 22, 1691.

on behalf of Monsieur l'Abbé in the quality of regular abbot and by virtue of the power of attorney [given to him] on the 27th of the same month.

On July 3[37] following, in the monastery of Saint Martin of Séez, of the Order of Saint Benedict, of the Congregation of Saint Maur,[38] Monsieur l'Abbé received the abbatial benediction from the hands of the Most Illustrious and Most Reverend Father in God Messire Patrick Plunkett, bishop of Ardagh in Ireland,[39] assisted by the abbot of this monastery and all the community.[40]

Having received the benediction that, for him, was not merely a simple ceremony but an increase in the graces God

---

[37] *Le trois Juillet*: the same date appears in the 1671 edition of the *Description*, but it is incorrect. All the biographers, from Pierre Le Nain and Armand-Jean Gervaise, through the *Gallia Christiana* and the two Louis Dubois, to Alban Krailsheimer, are agreed that the abbatial benediction took place not on the third but on July 13. Rancé entered La Trappe as its regular abbot the next day (for which Félibien gives the correct date).

[38] The ancient abbey of Saint-Martin in Sées had joined the reform movement of the Congregation of Saint-Maur—the Maurists—on July 13, 1636.

[39] Patrick Plunkett (1603–1679)—Félibien's "Patrice Plunquet"—was the cousin of Saint Oliver Plunkett, the last Roman Catholic martyr to die in England. Oliver was hanged, drawn, and quartered at Tyburn on July 1, 1681, and his preserved head, somewhat the worse for wear, is enshrined in Saint Peter's Church, Drogheda. Patrick Plunkett was the Cistercian abbot of Saint Mary's, Dublin, before being appointed bishop of Ardagh (1647–1669) and then bishop of Meath (1669–1679). From about 1652 to late 1664 he was away from Ireland because of Catholic persecution following the Cromwellian conquest of 1649–1653, which was why he was in Sées in July 1664 representing the bishop of Sées, who, at the time, was absent from his see. Plunkett died back home in Ireland on November 18, 1679, at the age of seventy-seven.

[40] According to Dubois, *Rancé*, 1:254, the bishop was assisted by Dom Bernard Ancelin, superior of the abbey, and Dom Albéric, a monk of Perseigne.

had given him, his only thought was how best to take advantage of the talents that had been entrusted to him, working toward his own salvation and that of his monks, of whom he had become the father and the shepherd. To this end he made his way to his abbey on the fourteenth day of that very month of July 1664. No sooner had he arrived there than he not only inspired his monks, by his natural eloquence, with a desire to become ever more perfect in the practices of the Strict Observance that they had embraced, but in a short time, he persuaded them so powerfully by his own example of undertaking all the austerities and penances that were used in establishing the Holy Rule [of Saint Benedict] that there was no monk who did not wish to imitate his abbot and, like him, to abstain from drinking wine[41] and eating eggs and fish,[42] and

---

[41] The *Regula S. Benedicti* 40.3 permits but does not prescribe a *hemina* of wine per person per day but adds that those who, by God's gift, can endure abstinence (*quibus autem donat Deus tolerantiam abstinentiae*) will have their own reward (40.4). Rancé, not surprisingly, adopts this stricter view. In Benedict's time, the *hemina* was a little less than ten fluid ounces (0.27 liters) or, in modern terms, somewhat less than half a bottle, a bottle being 0.75 litres or 25.4 fluid ounces. But by the Middle Ages the original meaning of *hemina* had been forgotten, and suggestions as to its true measure ranged from about a quarter of a liter to about three-quarters of a liter. The question was sensitive, and there was considerable controversy. A learned discourse with the title *Dissertation sur l'hémine de vin et sur la livre de pain de S. Benoist, & des autres anciens Religieux* was published anonymously in 1667 (first edition) and 1688 (second edition) by the Jansenist Claude Lancelot (1616–1695), solitary of Port-Royal and then Benedictine. A copy (we cannot tell of which edition) is recorded in the 1752 catalogue of the library of La Trappe: see Bell, *Library*, 391 (D.73).

[42] Rancé is here going beyond the Rule, which says simply that everyone, save for the sick who are very weak, must abstain entirely from eating the flesh of four-footed animals (*carnium quadrupedum*) (RB 39.11). But even the very sick, once their health improves, should abstain from meat as usual (36.9). The prohibition says nothing about eggs and obviously leaves the door open for the consumption of fish and poultry. Rancé is going back to the strict vegetarianism of the

adding three more hours each day to [the period devoted to] manual labor.[43] This was not only the [common] practice of

---

Desert Fathers, and Félibien discuses the diet at La Trappe below. Eggs might be served to the sick at La Trappe (though not in Lent or on the Monday or Tuesday preceding Ash Wednesday), but no one at all—sick or well—ate fish (*Constitutions*, 20; *Règlemens*, 19, 22 [III.6]).

[43] The hours for manual labor are set out in Chapter 48 of the *Regula S. Benedicti*. In the summer season (from Easter to October 1) the monks worked in the morning from the end of Prime (the first hour) to almost (*paene*) the fourth hour, and in the afternoon from the middle of the eighth hour until Vespers (48.3, 6). In the winter (from October 1 to the beginning of Lent) they worked from the end of Terce (the third hour) until None (the ninth hour), and during Lent from the third hour to the end of the tenth hour (48.11, 14). It is difficult to provide exact modern equivalents for these times since weight-driven mechanical clocks did not appear in Europe until the Middle Ages (the earliest surviving ones date from the fourteenth century), and the length of the hours varied from season to season in different locations. In Benedict and Bernard's time, the period from sunrise to sunset (and vice versa) was divided into twelve equal hours, which means that (except at the equinoxes of March 21 and September 21) a daytime summer hour was longer than a daytime winter hour. In late June in London, for example, a daytime hour lasted about eighty minutes while a nighttime hour lasted only forty. At Christmas the situation was reversed. By Rancé's time, mechanical clocks were commonplace and a day of twenty-four equal hours was standard, but the times of the Offices still differed in winter and summer (see Kinder, *Cistercian Europe*, 56). Rancé himself tells us that in summer Prime was at about 6 a.m. and the fourth hour was 10 a.m. at the Equinox, but sooner when the days are longer "selon nostre manière de compter" (Armand-Jean de Rancé, *Le Règle de saint Benoist nouvellement traduite, et expliquée selon son véritable esprit* [Paris: La veuve F. Muguet, 1703], 2:296). Benedict's "middle of the eighth hour" was 2.30 p.m., and the brothers worked "until the evening" (Rancé, *Le Règle*, 297). In winter, Terce was said at 9 a.m., and after Terce work continued until None at 3 p.m. (Rancé, *Le Règle*, 300). As Rancé says, the amount of time allotted by Benedict to manual labor was "considérable" (Rancé, *Le Règle*, 296): "Think about it, my brothers: there are almost six hours of this manual labor, save on the

the house, but there were many times when the whole community manifested a desire to commit itself forever to this practice by means of a special vow; but Monsieur l'Abbé judged it more advisable to have his monks keep [the Rule] with very great exactness and to spare them from making a particular vow to this effect.

Then, when he began to see the first seeds of virtue he had sown begin to germinate in this house, he was obliged to leave it on August 4, 1664, to go to Paris and take part in an assembly of abbots and superiors of the Strict Observance of Cîteaux that had been scheduled for the first of September[44] at the

---

shortest days" (Rancé, *Le Règle*, 301). The actual practice at La Trappe, however, appears to have been somewhat different. The manuscript *Explications sur La Règle du Bienheureux Père Saint Benoist ~ À L'usage de L'Abbaye de N. Dame de La Trappe*, 94 (preserved at La Trappe), tells us that although the monks would have preferred to follow Benedict's instructions to the letter, things have changed since his day and a number of Offices have been added to those noted in the Rule: the Office of the Dead, the Office of the Holy Virgin, and the celebration of High Masses. For this reason "it is almost impossible to give to each day more than three hours of manual labor." Félibien's summary of the constitutions of La Trappe relating to Manual Labor appear below (from n. 257).

[44] The complicated background to this and the next paragraph is the third phase of the War of the Observances. Cardinal Richelieu had supported the Strict Observance, and by the time of his death in 1643 the Abstinents had made considerable gains. In general, the Strict Observance looked to France for support while the Common Observance looked to Rome, but when Richelieu died the Common Observance immediately took advantage of the situation and elected Claude Vaussin, a former monk of Clairvaux and prior of Froidmont, to be abbot of the mother house of Cîteaux. His election was challenged on legal grounds by the Abstinents, and after a great deal of political wrangling, some of it fairly unsavory, the result was overturned and a new election called for May 1645. Vaussin was again the main contender, and his opponent was the Abstinent Jean Jouaud (see n. 25 above), but since Vaussin had twice as many supports as Jouaud, the result was a foregone conclusion. Vaussin was again

Collège des Bernardins.[45] Here, together with Monsieur l'Abbé

---

elected and his election hastily confirmed by both pope (Alexander VII) and king (Louis XIV). Once again the Strict Observance challenged the election, this time unsuccessfully, and Vaussin petitioned Louis to have the whole matter referred to Rome for papal arbitration. Louis agreed, and Vaussin set off for Rome, where he made the case to the pope that a just and necessary reform was one thing, but domination by the Strict Observance was quite another. Alexander then appointed a special Congregation for Cistercian Affairs and invited representatives from both Observances to Rome in the hope of finding some common ground. Jouaud was fully aware of the gravity of the situation and convoked an assembly of Abstinent leaders to meet at the Collège des Bernardins in Paris on September 1, 1664. This is the meeting to which Félibien is referring, and it was at this meeting that the thirty-two Abstinent abbots there present delegated Rancé and Dom Dominique Georges to be their representatives in Rome. See further Bell, *Rancé*, 62–65, for a brief account, and Lekai, *Rise*, 108–20 for the details. On the election of Claude Vaussin, see Louis J. Lekai, "The Election of Claude Vaussin as Abbot of Cîteaux," *Revue Bénédictine* 67 (1957): 202–19.

[45] The Collège des Bernardins or the Collège Saint-Bernard had been founded by Stephen Lexington in 1245 to house Cistercian students studying at the University of Paris. The church was much enlarged in the fourteenth century, and a final addition of four bays took place between 1510 and 1514. In the course of the seventeenth century, however, the upkeep of the church was neglected, and in the 1770s it was used as a cattle market before being demolished in 1859 to make way for Haussmann's new Paris. Happily, some of the claustral buildings (at 20, rue de Possy) still remain and were splendidly restored between 2004 and 2008. The history of the College has been well served in a number of articles by Louis Lekai in *Analecta Cisterciensia* 25 (1969): 180–208, 209–44; 26 (1970): 253–79; 28 (1972): 167–218; and *Cistercian Studies* 6 (1971): 172–79. See also Michael T. Davis, "Cistercians in the City: The Church of the *Collège Saint-Bernard* in Paris," in *Perspectives for an Architecture of Solitude. Essays on Cistercians: Art and Architecture in Honor of Peter Fergusson* (Cîteaux: Studia et Documenta, 13), ed. Terryl N. Kinder (Turnhout: Brepols and *Cîteaux—Commentarii cistercienses*, 2004), 223–34 (the illustration on p. 223 shows the college as Rancé would have seen it in August–September 1664).

of Val Richer,[46] he was delegated to go to Rome, there to present the feelings of the abbots and fathers of the Strict Observance with regard to the general reform of the Order of Cîteaux, which had to be discussed in conformity with the Brief of His Holiness.[47] The result of this was that after he had returned to his abbey and given control of it to Dom Jean Gaultier, the prior, and Dom Guillaume Kerviche, sub-prior,[48] he left [La Trappe for Rome] on the ninth of September.[49]

[46] The abbot of Val-Richer in Normandy was Dominique Georges (1613–1693), a learned man, who, like Rancé, embraced the monastic profession later in life (in 1652) after a distinguished career as a secular priest. He became the Strict Observance Visitor of the area in which La Trappe was to be found, made a visitation of the house on November 16, 1685, and submitted a most interesting report to the General Chapter in which he contrasted the state of affairs under Rancé with what had been the case when the latter entered on his regular abbacy (see n. 53 to the Introduction). He was a saintly and virtuous man, but it cannot be said that he was of great help to Rancé when the two were in Rome. His biography appeared three years after his death: Claude Buffier, *La Vie de M. l'abbé du Val-Richer, restaurateur de la discipline de ce monastère* (Paris: J. Boudot, 1696).

[47] This was the Apostolic Brief issued by Alexander VII on January 16, 1682. Its contents had clearly been influenced by Claude Vaussin and were generally unsympathetic to the Abstinent cause. See further Lekai, *Rise*, 114–15, with a summary of the Brief on p. 114.

[48] Guillaume Kerviche had been a monk at Perseigne before transferring to La Trappe. According to Dubois, *Histoire*, 130, he was professed on April 1, 1678, at the age of forty-five and died at La Trappe on February 1, 1689. Jean Gaultier, Gautier, or Gauthier appears as prior of La Trappe in Dubois, *Rancé*, 1:249, 301, but is not listed in Dubois's *Histoire* nor in the list of religious of La Trappe in [d'Arnaudin], *Le Vie de Dom Pierre Le Nain, religieux et ancient souprieur de l'abbayie de La Trappe* (Paris: La veuve Delaulne, 1741), 353–84.

[49] The first (1671) edition of the *Description* (p. 25) has September 19, which is incorrect. This is amended to the correct date, September 9, in the new edition of 1689. See Dubois, *Rancé*, 1:267–68.

Description of the Abbey of La Trappe (1689) 63

During his stay in Rome, where divine Providence[50] had not yet allowed that the good intentions of those who had delegated him and the solicitations he had made should have a happy result for the advantage of the Order,[51] God poured forth unceasingly new graces on the abbey of Our Lady of La Trappe. One often saw someone come to take the habit and embrace the austerity of their life, there to appear as a plant growing daily in virtues and bearing fruit in its season. The

---

[50] Providence was as important for Rancé as it was for all other seventeenth-century theologians, French and otherwise. It is, essentially, God's will in action, the Creator's total and beneficent control over all that happens in his creation. This does not mean, however, that we human beings are no more than puppets in God's hands, or that human beings may sit back and let Providence do all the work. Our business is to collaborate—literally to be colaborers or coworkers—with God's Providence, though in this cooperation God's work is always primary and ours always secondary. "You could not do better than submit yourself to God's guidance in everything," Rancé wrote to his sister, "and accept with complete resignation any difficulties that may come your way. It is enough to know that Providence rules everything, and that there is nothing that God does not do or permit for the sanctification of those who are his" (Letter 891013, quoted in Bell, *Understanding Rancé*, 92).

[51] This is Félibien's delicate way of saying that the Roman Mission was a failure. On the other hand, given the political situation in Rome and the tendency of the Curia to side with Claude Vaussin, there never had been any real hope of victory for the Strict Observance, and Jean Jouaud knew it. All that could be hoped for was a reasonable compromise. One of the most influential supporters of the Abstinent cause was the Queen Mother, Anne of Austria (her son was Louis XIV), but when she died on January 20, 1666, Rancé realized that there was no point in spending further time in Rome. He left the city on March 25 and eventually arrived in Paris on April 30. Here he reported to Jean Jouaud and the Abstinent leaders at the Collège des Bernardins, and—as Félibien says—finally arrived back ay La Trappe on May 10, 1666. He had been away some twenty months, and had not enjoyed his sojourn in the Holy City. See further Lekai, *Rise*, Chap. IX, "The Roman Arbitration" (119–31).

result was that when Monsieur l'Abbé returned from Rome on May 10, 1666, he not only had the solace of finding, on his return, more newly professed and his monastery living the same sort of life in which he had left it, but [he also found] all the monks so resolved never to abandon this [way of life] that when, during his absence, the prior had relaxed [the Rule] for a few days, wishing to have [the monks] served fish, they had all opposed this unanimously.[52]

From that time on, the austerity there was ever increased by the example of Monsieur l'Abbé, and the number of monks grew to such an extent that at present [1689] there are more than a hundred.[53] But [I know] you are amazed, Madame, that a house that has only five or six thousand pounds' income,

---

[52] See n. 42 above. The prior was Jean Gaultier (see n. 48). See further Dubois, *Rancé*, 1:304.

[53] I suspect that this is an exaggeration. In the first (1671) edition of the *Description*, Félibien reported the number as "more than forty" (p. 27). Five years later, on February 7, 1676, the community numbered forty-six: the abbot, twenty-seven choir monks, six novices, and twelve lay brothers (see Dubois, *Rancé*, 1:536; Dubois, *Histoire*, 28). By September 18, 1678, the number had increased by two (see Dubois, *Histoire*, 28), and six years later, in 1684, there were twenty-seven choir monks, eleven novices, and thirteen lay brothers, for a total of fifty-one, excluding the abbot (see Krailsheimer, *Rancé*, 102). Two years after that, in 1686, the number had increased to sixty-two, with seven more choir monks, one fewer novice, and five more lay brothers (Krailsheimer, *Rancé*, 102). In 1697 Claude Masson tells us that the *généreuse troupe* at the abbey comprised fifty professed monks and thirty-five to forty novices, without counting the lay brothers ([Claude Masson], *Deux retraites de dix jours contenant chacune trente Méditations, & un Sermon sur les principaux devoirs de la Vie Religieuse. Avec deux discours sur la Vie des Religieux de La Trape* [Lyon: Claude Bachelu, 1697], 441), so by this time the community might well have numbered more than a hundred. But if Félibien is correct, in the three years between 1686 and 1689 (the date of the new edition of the *Description*), the community at La Trappe must have increased by almost forty, and while that is not impossible, it seems to me improbable.

and where, in the past, six monks managed to live only with great difficulty,[54] can today support such a host, can maintain buildings that cost them much to keep in repair, and can still give alms and charity everywhere. I must therefore enter into the details of their life and tell you the way in which everything is conducted for the subsistence of the house, and where, truth to tell, save for the bread and some of their cider,[55] the monks themselves produce what food they need by the work of their own hands. I will therefore begin with the orderly way in which they receive visitors.

When someone has arrived at this abbey and crossed the Great Courtyard planted with fruit trees, of which I have spoken [earlier], he finds the door of the convent, where a religious of the house holds the office of Porter. When the latter has opened [the door], [the visitor] descends into a sort of vestibule[56] that is only twenty-four feet[57] in length and nine or ten feet wide. On the right is a room where guests are received, and on the left a large room where they eat. While the religious who has opened [the door] goes to advise Monsieur l'Abbé or Father Prior of the arrival of those who have entered, [the guests] wait in the [small] room where they can learn how they

---

[54] "In 1662, at the time of the Reform, the number of religious in the monastery had been reduced to seven individuals, of whom one was a lay brother" (Dubois, *Histoire*, 28). See further Dubois, *Rancé*, 1:255, and Krailsheimer, *Rancé*, 102.

[55] The portions of bread and cider will be discussed below.

[56] This is a somewhat abbreviated account. When guests arrived the porter would say *Deo gratias*, open the door, fall to his knees, and bow deeply before the visitors, say *Benedicite* by way of a greeting, and then show them into the little vaulted room and ask them for their patience while he went to announce their arrival to the Father Abbot (*Règlemens*, 102 [XV.2]).

[57] *quatre toises*: at this time and until 1812 a *toise* measured exactly six feet.

should comport themselves in this place, for there are little boards attached to the walls on which is written:

> We humbly request those whom Divine Providence[58] has brought to this monastery to find it appropriate for us to advise them of the following things:
>
> In the cloister one keeps perpetual silence. When one speaks in the places so designated or even in the gardens, one keeps one's voice as low as possible.
>
> One avoids, so far as is possible and at all times, any meeting with the religious, above all with any engaged in manual labor.
>
> If one needs anything in the monastery, one addresses oneself to the Porter, since the religious are strictly enjoined to be silent and can give no reply to those who speak to them.
>
> Servants[59] never enter the cloisters or the house.
>
> [Visitors] may never walk in the gardens between 11 o'clock and midday.[60]

In the vestibule, one can also read some passages taken from Holy Scripture. These are like the first announcements given to those who arrive, and very often [they form] the longest conversations that most strangers can have in this house, where one may say that the walls speak while the men say no word. For immediately on entering one sees these words of Jeremiah written on the door of the cloister:

---

[58] See n. 50 above.

[59] *Les domestiques,* that is to say, the servants of the guests, who could sometimes be numerous.

[60] The first four of these injunctions—from "We humbly request" to "those who speak to them"—correspond to the "Notices to be written in each room of the Guest House" in *Règlemens,* 105 (XVI). They do not appear in the *Constitutions.* All six are reproduced in Dubois, *Histoire,* 211–12.

SEDEBIT SOLITARIUS
ET TACEBIT.[61]

This is to make it known to those who aspire to the happiness of these solitaries that they should prepare themselves for withdrawal [from the world] and for silence. For this reason there is placed underneath [the above quotation] this passage from Job:

IN NIDULO MEO MORIAR,
ET SICUT PALMA MULTIPLICABO DIES MEOS.[62]

Strictly speaking, the only true solitaries who may be said to die in their house[63] are those who are placed in the situation of nevermore leaving it. And just as a palm tree that is never transplanted endlessly multiplies its branches and fruit, so the solitary increases the days of his happiness by cutting out from the course of his life those [days] that, unfortunately, he would have spent in the world.

On one side of the vestibule is written:

ELEGI ABJECTUS ESSE IN DOMO DEI MEI
MAGIS QUAM HABITARE IN
TABERNACULIS PECCATORUM.[64]

It appears that by these words of David these happy solitaries have wished to anticipate those who might ask them why they have left the world, [why they have] left so many of the goods and so many of the honors they [once] possessed in order to lead so austere a life and to abase themselves in tasks

---

[61] Lam 3:28: "He shall sit on his own and be silent."

[62] Job 29:18: "I shall die in my nest, and I shall multiply my days like a palm tree."

[63] *La Maison*, with an uppercase *M*, i.e., the abbey.

[64] Ps 83:11: "I have chosen to be abject in the house of my God rather than dwell in the tabernacles of sinners."

as servile as those in which they occupy themselves. So to ensure that their silence is never interrupted by such questions, they state clearly that they prefer to reduce themselves to a servile and abject condition so as to live in the house of God rather than living with greater splendor in the palaces of sinners. And they confess to God himself that a single day spent in the entrance hall of his palace is worth more than a thousand others that are never accompanied by this happiness, and it is this that is indicated on the other side of the vestibule by these words:

MELIOR EST DIES UNA IN
ATRIIS TUIS SUPER MILLIA.[65]

I mention these thoughts to you, Madame, that filled my spirit while awaiting the return of the Porter.

When the Father Prior or some other religious has come to receive the new guests, and after he has greeted them with

---

[65] Ps 83:11: "One day in your courts is better than a thousand [in the tabernacles of sinners]." Dubois, *Histoire*, 216–19, adds thirty more inscriptions that were to be found in various places in the abbey. The great majority are straightforward scriptural quotations, not always identified by Dubois, and a couple are taken from the Divine Office. Of the five others, *Citò a rectis ad prava, a pravis ad praecipitia, si liceat, transcurritur* is based on Gaius Velleius Paterculus, *Res gestae divi Augusti*, 2.3.4 and 2.10 (but it seems to have been a well-known saying); *Si incipis, perfectè incipe* is ps.-Bernard/William of Saint-Thierry, *Epistola ad fratres de Monte Dei* 4.11; PL 184:315B; SCh 223:174 (§39); *Verò pro nobis hostia erit, Deo cum nosmetipsos hostiam fecerimus* is ps-Hugh of Saint-Victor, *Sermones centum, sermo* 50; PL 177:1042D; *Vindicari vis Christianus* (sic, for *Christiane*): *nondum vindicatus est Christus* is Augustine, *Enar. in Ps.* 30, II, *sermo* 3.12; PL 36:255; *Quamvis sis in tuto, noli esse securus* is ps.-Bernard, *De ord. vitae et morum instit.* 12.40; PL 184:583A; and *O beata solitudo! O sola beatitudo!* was attributed to a number of classical and medieval writers (including Bernard of Clairvaux), but there is no clear evidence for it before the sixteenth century.

great humility and deep prostrations, he takes them into the cloister and conducts them to the church, there to adore the Holy Sacrament. Returning from there, they enter either the small chamber or the large room, and while they wait for their meal, a religious reads a chapter from the *Imitation [of Christ]*.[66]

What is served at the table of the guests is similar to that given to the religious; that is to say, they eat only the same vegetables and the same bread, and they drink cider just as in the refectory. The usual dishes are soup, two or three plates of vegetables, and a plate of eggs, which is the extraordinary portion for visitors.[67] They are never served fish, even though

---

[66] According to the *Règlemens*, 103 (XV.2), the porter, after bowing deeply to the guests or kneeling before them, leads them into the church, where he first gives them Holy Water and then stands a little behind them while they make their prayers. He then takes them to their apartment, where he reads to them from "some book of piety." Thomas à Kempis's *Imitation of Christ* is not mentioned, though there is no reason to doubt the accuracy of Félibien's account. Not only was the book hugely popular at this time (it appeared in innumerable editions), not only was it a volume specifically permitted for reading by Rancé's monks (see Dubois, *Rancé*, 2:313), but it was also one of Rancé's three favorites. The other two were the Lives of the Desert Fathers and Cardinal Bellarmine's *Art of Dying Well* (see Mary A. Schimmelpenninck, *A Tour to Alet and La Grande Chartreuse by Dom Claude Lancelot, Author of the Port Royal Grammars*, 2nd ed. [London: J. &. A. Arch, 1816], 2:327). In his third Conference for the first Sunday in Lent, Rancé tells us that in addition to Scripture, "we add the book of *The Imitation of Jesus Christ*, and still some other for help and instruction" (Armand-Jean de Rancé, *Conférences ou Instructions sur les Epîtres et Évangiles des Dimanches et Principales Festes de l'Année, et sur les Vestures & Professions Religieuses. Tome second* [Paris: F. Delaulne, 1720], 240).

[67] "[Guests] are treated respectfully, but are only served the food common to all in the refectory. The only additions to this are eggs and butter" (*Règlemens*, 104 [XV.4]). "Extraordinary" here means literally "out of the ordinary," i.e., something beyond what was normally served to the monks.

the ponds may be full of them. Sometimes people who are unwell are given wine.[68]

During the whole of the meal [a religious] continues to read the *Imitation [of Christ]*, but this has been the case for only a short time. Previously, [the reader] began only a single chapter, and after he had read two or three sentences, the Father Prior or the religious who was there to look after the guests (for he never eats with them) stopped the reading, and [the guests] were then free to talk of various things. But since they sometimes threw out questions that, because the different ideas of those who were there could give rise to arguments and useless disputes, Monsieur l'Abbé (who has great foresight) found a way to prevent these occasions by having a reading for the entire time they are at table, and after that each person retires to the room appointed for him.

Visitors have their own special suite of rooms, which looks out on the Courtyard, and they never enter the cloisters except to go to the church at the times of the Offices. Not long ago they used to eat in the refectory, but when Monsieur l'Abbé saw that the frequent visits from worldly people could distract the spirit of his religious who had entered this solitude only to withdraw from dealings with seculars, he wisely resolved to admit only a few visitors in the future, and only those whom he well knew could not distract his religious in any way. He himself is at present more withdrawn [from the world] than ever and does not speak to all those who come to see him; [if he did], he could eventually find himself having to respond to too many people who would steal from him the time of his retreat. And although there is scarcely any [visitor] who does

---

[68] Wine was never served to the religious in the refectory, nor even in the infirmary for *foiblesse*, which we might translate as chronic weakness. But a little could be administered as a remedy if someone fainted (*Constitutions*, 19; *Règlemens*, 20 [III.6], 88 [XII.13]). See n. 223 below.

not wish to ask his advice, he will not interrupt the Offices or his other obligations for anyone, for in his view his first obligation is to work for his own salvation and to guide his religious, and he therefore excuses himself from any other duties one may ask of him.

For this reason he had begun [to build] a dwelling for himself by the side of the church, separated from the other apartments, so that there he could be more withdrawn.[69] But the continual needs that the religious have of him, and his own vigilance in guiding them, meant that he had to leave the building unfinished so that he could live among them and, in this way, be always ready to comfort them on all those occasions when his ministry was needed and unceasingly provide them with the spiritual nourishment so necessary for souls wholly detached from the world.

At this point, Madame, I could speak to you of the other buildings in the abbey of La Trappe, but the plan I sent you will give you some sense of how they are laid out.[70] You must know only that nowhere in the entire monastery will you see anything magnificent or that which titillates the senses.[71] The church has nothing of significance save the holiness of the place. It is built in the gothic style and is most unusual, for

---

[69] At the southwest corner of the church: Building no. 32 on **Figure 1**. This paragraph on the unfinished *logement* for Rancé does not appear in the 1671 edition of the *Description*.

[70] The plan from the 1689 edition is reproduced as **Figure 1**.

[71] I have translated *curiosité* as "that which titillates the senses." In seventeenth-century French, *curieux* does not mean "curious" in the usual modern sense, but refers to writings that stimulate and pander to our human curiosity, and *curiosité* was roundly condemned by a multitude of monastic writers, including Bernard, as being both useless and dangerous. See Richard Newhauser, "The Sin of Curiosity and the Cistercians," in *Erudition at God's Service: Studies in Medieval Cistercian History, XI*, ed. John R. Sommerfeldt (Kalamazoo, MI: Cistercian Publications, 1987), 71–95.

the end of the choir seems to represent the stern of a ship.[72] But this must not be taken for some noble and subtle invention of the architect, since all the workmanship is crude and even contrary to the rules of art. There is nothing majestic or splendid about this church: it is neither too dark nor too light. In size it is 132 feet long by 54 feet wide[73] or thereabouts. The aisles that encircle it are 12 feet wide.[74] A high railing divides the church in two and prevents anyone from entering from the choir side of the nave. In the area closed off by the railing there are two altars under the crucifix, and it is here that Masses are said for male visitors, who stay in the lower end of the church. Women are not permitted to enter [the church], but there is a chapel in the outer courtyard[75] where Mass is said for them on Sundays and feast days. This enclosed area in front of the crucifix also serves as the choir for the lay brothers, and between

---

[72] As we saw in the Introduction, Prince William the Aetheling, the only legitimate son of Henry I of England, was drowned when the White Ship struck a rock and sank off Barfleur on November 25, 1120. At the same time, the wife of Rotrou III, count of Mortagne, also perished, together with about a dozen members of his family, and Rotrou built a memorial chapel to his wife's memory (see also n. 15 above), which was the beginning of La Trappe. According to the *Memoriale* of the foundation of the abbey, dated 1385—a document that is not always reliable—the roof of Rotrou's church took the form of an overturned boat so as always to commemorate the unhappy reason for its foundation (see the *Memoriale fundationis hujus abbatiæ* in Dubois, *Histoire*, 285). Whether this was actually the case has been called into question—it may be simply pious after-wit—though in Félibien's time the roof of the church certainly had the appearance of an overturned skiff. For an illustration, see *Iconographie de l'abbaye de La Trappe des origines à 1900 précédée de l'iconographie de l'abbé de Rancé, réformateur de ce monastère (1664–1700)*, Cahiers Percherons (Association des Amis du Perche) 39 (1973): 64.

[73] Twenty-two *toises* by nine *toises*: see n. 57 above.

[74] The aisles can be seen on the plan of the church (Building no. 15 in **Figure 1**).

[75] Building no. 1 in **Figure 1**.

Description of the Abbey of La Trappe (1689) 73

this choir and that of the monks there is another space that serves as a choir for those who are sick. The monks' choir is furnished with thirty-six upper stalls and thirty lower stalls.[76] The high altar is very simple: its lower part is of stone, on which is carved, in a very old style, Our Savior on the cross and the twelve apostles. In the middle of the lintel that is built over it and that serves for a frieze there is a representation of an altar on which is a flaming fire with a kneeling angel on each side. Below this[77] is the statue of the Virgin standing upright holding her Son on her left arm, and in her right hand is a little pavilion under which is suspended the Holy Sacrament in accordance with the ancient custom of the church.[78] Under this statue on the pedestal that supports it is written [in Greek] ΘΕΟΤΟΚΩ [THEOTOKŌ], that is to say, "To the Mother of God."[79]

However holy and august are the ceremonies of the church, there are always those who seek only to find there something to criticize. You therefore come across those who want to find fault with this sort of suspension [for the Holy Sacrament] and have it pass for a novelty, and even as something injurious to the honor of the Virgin, to have her image serve to carry the holy ciborium. But such people are ignorant of the fact that this is in accordance with the ancient practice of the Order of Saint Benedict, for in the past the holy sacrament was supported in just the same way by the statue of the Virgin on the high altar at Cîteaux. It is only recently that this usage has been changed in the monasteries of this Order, with tabernacles being placed on altars—a practice that was introduced [only]

[76] These can be seen in **Figure 2** (p. 27), the lower stalls in front of the higher.

[77] Félibien actually says "above," but he is referring to the altar table, not the lintel over it.

[78] See **Figure 2**.

[79] For another description of the statue and the suspended ciborium, see Dubois, *Rancé*, 1:619–20.

a short time ago.⁸⁰ You might even say that it would be a sort of impiety not to wish that the statue of the Virgin should serve to support the Holy Sacrament, since faith obliges us to believe that the sacred body of Jesus Christ is there present in its reality, and that the greatest honor that the Holy Mother could receive would be to carry it still: she whose whole glory and happiness was to carry [that body] in her womb and suckle it at her breasts.

Also, Monsieur l'Abbé himself, as if anticipating this offence that would be so injurious not only to the Mother but also to the Son, composed these two couplets in which he displayed the honor the Virgin receives by still bearing today the glorious body of her Son, and that she alone is worthy of such a holy task.

> *Si quaeras natum cur matris dextera gestat.*
> *Sola fuit tanto munere digna parens.*
> *Non poterat fungi majori munere mater,*
> *Nec poterat major dextera ferre Deum.*⁸¹

---

⁸⁰ The custom of placing the tabernacle on an altar, though not at first the high altar, dates, effectively, from the early sixteenth century, when Matteo Giberti (1495–1543), bishop of Verona, instructed the priests of his diocese to place the receptacle on an altar. Saint Charles Borromeo (1538–1584) also moved the tabernacle from the sacristy to an altar in his cathedral of Milan, though once again, not the high altar, and the custom spread rapidly through northern Italy. In 1614 Pope Pius V required the relocation of the tabernacle in all churches in the diocese of Rome. The placing of the tabernacle on the high altar came about in reaction to the Protestant Reformation and the Protestant denial of the doctrine of transubstantiation. When the Catholic faithful saw the tabernacle on the high altar, what they were seeing was the Real Presence, the very substance of the Body of Christ. Félibien is quite correct, therefore, in maintaining that the custom was introduced into Cistercian churches in what, for him, was the recent past.

⁸¹ "If you ask why the Mother bears the Son on her right arm, / It is because this Mother alone was worthy of such a great honor; / No

On the altar there is only a small ebony crucifix, and at the two ends of the altar table there are two small wooden shelves from which come two projections supporting two candles that are lit only during Mass. On feast days these are doubled, so that instead of two candles there are four. There are also two other [candles] in front of the nearest pillars, which are lit at the elevation [of the Host]. There are no silver candlesticks or other rich ornaments; neither the chasubles nor even the altar frontals are made of silk, though there may be a few [silk ones] that were used in the past. Since Monsieur l'Abbé seeks only to conform in all things to the spirit of the first founders of the Order, and especially of Saint Bernard—he who railed so strongly against monks who adorn their churches with silver and who would make them spectacles of worldly splendor[82]—he strives as much as possible to retain in all things this simplicity and this mark of poverty so becoming to monks, which ought to be their unique lot. It is also true that this church, by its simplicity, inspires much more devotion than many others where the altars are laden with rich candlesticks and precious vessels, and the odor poured forth by the continual and fervent prayers of these good monks is a perfume more agreeable to

---

other mother could have rendered a greater service, / No arm was more worthy to carry God." The couplets are elegiac couplets—a hexameter followed by a pentameter—and a more literal translation is as follows: "If you should ask why the mother's right hand bears the child, / [It is because] she alone was a parent worthy of such an office; / No mother could have performed a greater office, / No greater right hand could have carried God." In other words, Mary was bearing Christ with both her arms: with her left arm she bore the physical body of the infant Jesus, and with her right the eucharistic Body of Christ. For a full account of Rancé's devotion to the Mother of God, see David N. Bell, "Armand-Jean de Rancé (1626–1700) and the Mother of God: A Re-evaluation of His Position, with a Translation of His *Conference for the Feast of the Nativity of the Virgin*," *CSQ* 48 (2013): 39–78.

[82] See Bernard, *Apologia* 11.28; SBOp 3:104–6.

God than all this incense and these thuribles smoking away in other places. And it is of their way of praying, Madame, that I must speak to you now, so that I may tell you how these happy anchorites live in this monastery where all their actions are a continual prayer to God.

In summer they sleep for eight hours and in winter for seven. They get up at two o'clock in the morning to go to Matins, which normally lasts up to four and a half hours, for besides the main Office, they always begin with [the Office of] the Virgin, and between [this and the main Office] there is half an hour's meditation.[83] On days when the Church does not celebrate the festival of any saint, they still recite the Office of the Dead. In summer, when they come out from Matins, they can go and rest in their cells[84] until Prime, but in winter they

---

[83] On the 2 a.m. time for rising, see n. 199 below. The Office of the Virgin is the Little Office of the Blessed Virgin Mary, which seems to have originated as a monastic devotion in the mid-eighth century. By the end of the tenth century its use was widespread, and it became ever more widespread in the centuries that followed. The text was standardized by Pope Pius V in 1585. It is not quite clear how long Matins lasted, and it is difficult to reconcile Félibien's statement that it began at 2 a.m. and could last up to four and a half hours, with the beginning of Prime at 5.30 a.m. There was, however, some flexibility as to when Matins began and ended, and this also depended on whether it was summer or winter, a feria or a saint's day. Furthermore, what Félibien says is that Matins could last "up to (*jusque à*)" four and a half hours, not that it necessarily did so, and we read in the *Règlemens* that it is better to start the office an hour early than to end it a quarter of an hour late (*Règlemens*, 2 [I.1]).

[84] Rancé's intention was always to return to the *premier esprit* of the Rule of Saint Benedict (see n. 23 above), which calls for a common dormitory, but by the seventeenth century the principle of individual cells in a partitioned dormitory was too firmly entrenched to be changed. The Regulations make it clear that each cell had a door (which was never to be left open) and a window, and contained a bed, a table, various images, clothing, and a chamber pot. Each cell was to be swept twice a week, and candles or lamps were permitted only in the cells of the superior, cellarer, sacristan, and the religious

go into a common chamber near the warming room, where each one reads on his own. The priests nearly always take this time to say Mass, and Monsieur l'Abbé often waits in the church for their confessions. For as well as being the father of these monks, he is also their confessor.

At half-past five they say Prime, which lasts a good half hour. Then they go into Chapter, where they stay about another half hour, except on certain days when they stay there longer. On these days Monsieur l'Abbé gives them an instructive sermon.[85] At seven o'clock they go to work. That is to say, each one takes off his outer habit, which they call a cowl, and tucking up [the tunic] they wear beneath it,[86] some take themselves off to till the ground, others to riddle it, and yet others to carry stones. Each one accepts his task without either choice or preference as to what he should do. Monsieur l'Abbé himself is the first at work, and it is he who turns his hands to the most servile and arduous tasks rather than [delegating them] to anyone else. When the weather prevents them from working outside, they clean the church, scour the vessels [used in the liturgy], do the washing, and peel the vegetables. Sometimes

---

who was in charge of the clock. See *Règlemens*, 10–14 (II), and David N. Bell, "Chambers, Cells, and Cubicles: The Cistercian General Chapter and the Development of the Private Room," in Kinder, *Perspectives for an Architecture of Solitude*, 187–98.

[85] *Des doctes Prédications*, which we would normally translate as "learned sermons." But given Rancé's antipathy to what he regarded as unnecessary learning and his restrictions on what books a monk should read, it seems to me that we should here translate *docte* as "instructive." If anyone wishes to read a complete translation of one of Rancé's instructive sermons, his Conference on the Nativity of the Virgin and his Conference on Spiritual Joy are both available in English (see n. 81 above and n. 90 below). See further Bell, *Library*, 63–69; and David N. Bell, "Bread of Angels: Armand-Jean De Rancé on the Eucharist with a Translation of his Conference for the Feast of Corpus Christi," *CSQ* 52, no. 3 (2017): 277–309.

[86] This is an abbreviated account of the instructions in *Règlemens*, 63 (X.1). The tunic was never to be raised above the knees.

there are two or three of them sitting on the ground side by side digging up root vegetables, but never talking among themselves. There are also some places intended for work under cover where many monks are occupied, some with writing [liturgical] books for the church, others with binding them;[87] some [are busy] with carpentry, others with making pots. Thus [they are employed] in a variety of useful occupations, for there is hardly anything necessary for the house or for their own use that they do not make themselves. But they never apply themselves to any work that is too absorbing,[88] something in which the mind could find too much pleasure, for one of the maxims of this worthy abbot is that whoever has retired into solitude to possess nothing more than God should never turn aside from this [end] to become fondly attached to vain things. Instead, he should stay continually united to God, ever maintaining himself in the love of this Supreme Beauty, which should be the object of all his desires.

When they have worked an hour and a half, they go to the Office, which begins at half-past eight. They say Terce and, following that, Mass and Sext. What is worthy of consideration

---

[87] For seventeenth-century manuscripts written at and for La Trappe, see David N. Bell, "The Manuscripts of La Trappe," *Cîteaux— Commentarii cistercienses* 55 (2004): 87–153, *passim,* and Bell, *Library,* 101–7.

[88] Lit. "They do not apply themselves to any *curieux ouvrage,*" i.e., to any work that engages and stimulates the brain. The principle is precisely that of the Desert Fathers, who commonly made their living by weaving cloth and making baskets—repetitive tasks that could easily go hand-in-hand with prayer and meditation. This could, of course, have unfortunate consequences: "It was said of [John the Dwarf] that he wove the matting for two baskets into one without thinking about it, his spirit being absorbed in contemplation" (Marius Chaîne, *Le Manuscrit de la version copte en dialecte sahidique des "Apophthegmata Patrum"* [Cairo: L'Institut française d'archéologie orientale, 1960], 17 [§84]).

is the way the monks perform the Office, for you see them chanting the praises of God with steady voices and solemn tones, but above all with so devout an air that it is easy to conclude that it is with their hearts much more than their mouths that they chant these divine songs with which they make the church resound, and I confess to you that there is nothing that touches the heart, [nothing] that raises the spirit more to God than to hear them chanting at Matins. For since their church is lit by only a single lamp in front of the high altar (except for the great feast days when a [second] is lit in the center of the monks' choir, and a [third] before the Crucifix), the darkness, joined with the silence, causes the soul to be filled with the sacred unction poured forth in all their psalms, and then, penetrated by these burning arrows that come forth from the depths of their hearts, [the soul] feels itself sweetly enflamed with the same love that consumes them. Their chant is expressive and pleasant, and whether they be seated or whether they be standing, whether they be kneeling or whether they be prostrate, it is with such profound humility that one sees clearly that they are subject much more to the spirit than the body. However self-effacing[89] their bearing, and whatever the degree of their humility, one never sees on their faces any sign of sadness or despondency, nor [any sign] of affectation or constraint in any of their actions. Joy is poured forth everywhere,[90] and their voices, their free and natural actions, clearly show the pleasure they feel in this holy exercise, and with how much love they carry out all the duties of their Rule.

---

[89] *Modeste*, which one might also translate as "unassuming." The word had a stronger meaning than our present-day "modest."

[90] Félibien is not exaggerating, though joy and penance may at first glance seem odd companions. The matter is discussed in David N. Bell, "Armand-Jean de Rancé: A Conference on Spiritual Joy," CSQ 37 (2002): 33–46.

When they have said Sext they retire to their cells until half-past ten[91]—that is to say, for about half an hour—during which time they may devote themselves to some reading.[92] After that, they go into the church to chant None. If, however, it is one of the Church's fast days, the Office is delayed and None is said shortly before midday. They then go to the refectory.

---

[91] The 1671 edition reads "half-past two" but *deux* (two) is merely a typographical error for *dix* (ten).

[92] This is contrary to the 1690 Regulations, which state that reading is not to be done in one's cell, but only in the cloister or chapter room: see *Règlemens*, 11–12 (II.3) and 34 (V.11). Nevertheless, Félibien repeats the statement that the monks might read in their cells at nn. 98 and 100 below, and, in 1671, that was certainly the case. It was, in fact, the common practice in the Cistercian Order in the seventeenth century, but in 1689—the date of the new edition of the *Description*—it was no longer correct. By that time Rancé had reverted to the ancient Usages of the Order, which permitted such reading only in the cloister or, in winter, in the chapter room (see *Ecclesiastica officia* 71.5–7 and 74.3; Choisselet/Vernet, 212, 216). To this end, in 1672 Rancé began the restoration of the cloister adjoining the church, and the work was completed in 1675. The first time it was used for common reading was at 2 p.m. on All Saints' Day (see Pierre Le Nain, *La Vie du Révérend Père Dom Armand-Jean Le Boutillier de Rancé, abbé et réformateur de la Maison-Dieu Nôtre-Dame de la Trappe* [Paris: F. Delaulne, 1719], 1:167–68). From that time on, the cells were to be used only for sleeping (see Dubois, *Rancé*, 1:517–18). By "reading" Félibien means *lectio divina*, the meditative, ruminative reading of some suitable text—the works of the Fathers, for example, or the writings of Saint Bernard—designed not to supply intellectual information, but to produce spiritual transformation. For an excellent account, see Duncan Robertson, *Lectio Divina: The Medieval Experience of Reading*, CS 238 (Collegeville, MN: Cistercian Publications, 2011). For Rancé's views on the nature and importance of *lectio divina*, see the very sound article by Marie-Raphaël Vallet, "La *lectio divina* selon Rancé," in *Tamié 79. La Lectio Divina. Rencontre des Pères-Maîtres et Mères-Maîtresses bénédictins et cisterciens du Nord et de l'Est de la France à l'abbaye de Tamié (Savoie) du 22 au 27 janvier 1979* (n.p.; n.d.), 302–35; English translation as "*Lectio* according to Rancé," *Liturgy O.C.S.O.* 22, no. 2 (1988): 21–75.

It is there, Madame, that you may see the frugality, or rather the very same austerity, of the first solitaries. The refectory is very large, and there is a long row of tables on each side. That of Monsieur l'Abbé is in the center [at the east end] facing these and has places for six or seven people. He himself sits at one end with the Father Prior next to him on his left, and when there are visitors eating in the refectory (which, at present, is hardly ever the case), [they sit] on his right. The tables are bare, without tablecloths, but very clean. Each monk has his own napkin, his earthenware cup, his knife, and his boxwood spoon and fork, which are always put in the same place. They have before them just as much bread as they may eat, a jug of water, and another jug holding about half a liter[93] of cider—but [only] filled to a little more than halfway.[94] The reason for this is that what would be needed to fill up [the jug] is kept aside for their collation,[95] since they may have no more than a total of half a liter [of cider] a day. Their bread is greyish-brown and very coarse, for they may never sift their flour: it is merely passed through a riddle, and, consequently, almost all the bran remains. And if this is not the practice in all the monasteries of this same Order, it is, nevertheless, one of the points of the ancient Rule of Cîteaux,[96] which is observed to the letter in this

---

[93] Lit. "about a *chopine* of Paris," which measured 0.4656 liters.

[94] Wine was never served in the refectory (see n. 68 above), for "we use only cider or beer, and we never provide more than a *chopine*, measure of Paris, at each meal" (*Règlemens*, 21 [III.6]).

[95] Collation, at 5 p.m., was the light snack taken at the end of fast days after Vespers and before Compline. Collation was always accompanied by a reading, traditionally from the Lives of the Desert Fathers, especially as arranged by John Cassian in his *Collationes Patrum* or "Collections [of Sayings] of the Fathers." This was probably the origin of the term *collation*, though the readings were never restricted to Cassian and included a wide variety of patristic texts. See further n. 224 below.

[96] *Instituta Generalis Capituli*, XIV, "De pane quotidiano," dating from about 1147, stipulates that "the bread in our monasteries shall

house. They are served a soup that is sometimes made with herbs, at other times with peas or lentils, and, in like manner, they will now have herbs, now vegetables, with two small portions on fast days, namely, a little plate of lentils with another of spinach or beans or gruel or oatmeal or carrots or some other root vegetables—whatever is available according to the season—for they do not seek to have different dishes at every meal. Their soups are always without butter and without oil, and in other dishes they use [butter and oil] only very rarely, and never at all on the fast days of the Church. Their normal sauces are made with salt and water thickened with a little wheat flour[97] and sometimes a little milk, but in truth, they use so little of the latter when they make cabbage- or pumpkin-soup that the water is merely whitened. Indeed, they do not use [milk] at all when they are abstaining from butter and oil, and then they make their gruel with no more than flour, water, and salt. When they are served beetroots, I have noticed that each religious is offered oil in a small bowl: some take a little of it with their spoon; others content themselves with eating [the beetroots] only with salt and vinegar. There are also certain vegetables, such as artichokes and asparagus, which seem to them to be too dainty, and these are never served at their tables and never grown in their garden. For dessert they are given two apples or two pears, cooked or raw.

When all the monks and lay brothers are in the refectory, the porter brings the keys of the convent to Monsieur l'Abbé. The only ones who eat after the others are the one who does the cooking, the one who serves at table, and the one who gives the reading during the meal. When these good monks have been filled in this way, both in body and soul, they give thanks to God and go to the church to complete their prayers. On leaving the church they retire to their cells, where they may

---

not be white, not even on major feasts, but coarse (*grossus*), that is, made with bran (*cum cribro*)" (Waddell, *Texts*, 330–31, 461–62).

[97] *Gruau*, which might also be translated as "hulled grain."

apply themselves to reading[98] and contemplation, and in this they are not hampered by the fog of wine or [rich] foods that fill the brain with heavy clouds and render the spirit incapable of any meditation after the meal. Sometimes, too, they use this time to speak with Monsieur l'Abbé when they have something to disclose to him regarding the state of their soul. They go to him as to a source of living and beneficial water by which they are refreshed, and they never leave him without being strengthened and filled with new graces. For I will tell you here in passing that when they enter the novitiate, they begin by making a general confession to him to reveal the depths of their conscience, and thereafter they make their confession to no other but him. It is in this way that he knows their spirit perfectly, that he sees whether they have a true vocation to embrace the austere life of this house, and that he judges their capacity for the tasks he intends for them. The especial care that he takes for the conduct of their souls in no way offends or constrains them. Indeed, it is so much to their taste that they find it difficult to make their confession to anyone else, even when he gives them leave to do so. And even if he is so rigorous in correcting them that, in public, he appears too severe, he nevertheless addresses all their specific concerns with so great a love and tenderness that they never find greater joy than when they can converse with him.

At one o'clock or thereabouts, [a bell] summons them to go to work, either taking up where they left off in the morning or beginning some other [task]. In this way, twice a day they fulfill this precept of Scripture, which does not wish anyone to eat who has not earned his food by his own work.[99] And as they themselves till the soil so as to live by the work of their own hands, the first water with which they water it is the sweat of their brow.

---

[98] See n. 92 above.
[99] 2 Thess 3:10: "If anyone does not wish to work, neither shall he eat."

After an hour and a half of work, or sometimes two hours, the bell is rung to end [manual labor]. At this time each one takes off his clogs, puts his tools back in their proper place, retrieves his cowl, and retires to his room to read[100] or meditate until Vespers, which are said at four o'clock. [Vespers] lasts about three-quarters of an hour, and at five o'clock they go to the refectory, where each monk finds for his collation four ounces of bread, the rest of his half-liter of cider (so the total is less than a *septier*[101]), and two pears or two apples, or some nuts on fast days [as specified] in the Rule.[102] But on the fast days of the Church they are given only two ounces of bread and only one [of the two portions of] drink.[103] On days when they are not fasting, they have for their supper the rest of their cider, a portion of root vegetables, and some bread, just as at dinner, with an apple or pear for dessert. In the morning, however, they are given only one portion of vegetables with their soup. When they take only collation, a quarter of an hour is

---

[100] See n. 92 above.

[101] How much is a *septier*? At the time Félibien was writing, it was a measure of both dry and liquid capacity, as well as of land, and differed significantly from place to place and, indeed, from material to material. The *septiers* for grain, oats, salt, and charcoal were all different, and there were at least three dozen variants depending on whether you were in Abbeville or in Vitry-sur-Marne. As a liquid measure, it was used almost entirely for wine and, once again, could vary wildly in quantity. In Paris a *septier* of wine was more than seven liters, in Montpellier almost thirty-four liters. But lest we think of Rancé's monks prostrate after consuming gallons of cider, the *septier* was also a synonym for the *chopine*. In other words, what Félibien is saying is that in the course of the day the monks of La Trappe never consumed more than about half a liter of cider. Whether they had free access to water is mentioned neither by Félibien nor by the *Constitutions* or the *Règlemens*.

[102] See *Règlemens*, 21 (III.6). Nuts are not mentioned in the Rule of Saint Benedict.

[103] I.e., half of a half-liter of cider, which is less than eight fluid ounces, or less than one cup in modern culinary terms.

enough for them, so that they still have half an hour to themselves, after which they make their way into the chapter room, where they read some devotional book until six o'clock, at which time they go [into the church] to say Compline. Following that they meditate for half an hour. When they leave the church, after being sprinkled with holy water at the hand of Monsieur l'Abbé, they enter the dormitory, and at seven o'clock [the bell] summons them to retire. Each then goes to his bed: that is to say, each of them lies down fully clothed on boards, on which there is a prickly[104] straw mattress, a pillow stuffed with straw, and a coverlet, for they never undress, even when they are ill. The only concession that they receive in the infirmary is that their straw mattresses are not prickly. On rare occasions certain invalids may be provided with linen, save in cases where the illness is unusual or wholly exceptional. For the rest, they are carefully tended, and eat eggs and butchers' meat, though poultry is never served, any more than preserved or sugared fruits.

But I must not forget to say that those bodily infirmities that, in other monasteries, are a great obstacle to the profession of a novice, are here a mark of his vocation. Monsieur l'Abbé never refuses them because they are prone to some illness or other, for he has no fear that the community may be inconvenienced by them, nor that they might not become monks, since Christian charity[105] obliges them to help one another, and that

---

[104] The word is *piquée*, which means both stitched and prickly (from the verb *piquer*), but the comment that follows—that the only concession to the monks in the infirmary was that their mattresses were not *piquées*—clearly indicates the latter.

[105] Generally speaking, *amour* is the generic term for love and may refer to all forms of love, good or bad, properly directed or misdirected, spiritual or carnal alike. *Charité*, however, always refers to love that is properly directed. Augustine provides an exact definition: "I call charity a movement of the soul towards the enjoyment of God [*ad fruendum Deo*] for his own sake, and of oneself and one's neighbor for the sake of God" (*De doctrina Christiana* 3.16; PL 34:72). This is the

far from fleeing from suffering, they should embrace all forms of discomfort, and even seek opportunities to suffer more. In his view, those who enter this house come there only to mortify their flesh and render it obedient to the spirit by fasting and discipline. And since there is no greater mark of God's mercy on human beings than to be afflicted by illnesses, the latter is a testimony that they are specially called by God, since he himself puts them in this way so as to purify them and lead them to that holiness of life that the others try to acquire through austerities. But what [Monsieur l'Abbé] considers most is the interior disposition of their soul, taking great care [to be sure] that they are truly obedient and truly dedicated to God.[106] He never receives any who cultivate society or idle away their lives in vain and frivolous pursuits, for fear that even one such person might corrupt all those who have embraced the [monastic] life in order to think on God alone.

Such, Madame, is the way of life of these solitaries, and such are the practices with which they fill this emptiness and all those moments that worldly people often find so long and tedious, and that lead them to seek all manner of diversions so that they may spend their lives (which yet seem to them to be so short) with as little concern as possible. I have no doubt that life [at La Trappe] appears frightful to them when they hear of this renunciation of all pleasures, this mortification and austerity in eating and drinking, and the almost continual fasting—[fasting] that is so rigorous that (when you recall what I have told you of the nature of each meal), that for most of the year the body supports itself for twenty-four hours on no more

---

charity of which Saint Paul speaks in 1 Cor 13:4-8, and when Félibien uses the word, I have almost always translated it as *charity*.

[106] Lit. "and strongly recollected [*fort recüeillis*]." Recollection—*recueillement*—is an important technical term in seventeenth-century French spirituality. It involves the deliberate withdrawal of the mind and intellect from outward earthly things in order to focus them on the inward presence of God in the soul. Hence my paraphrase: "truly dedicated to God."

than two pears or two apples, together with a tiny morsel of bread, even though they are at manual labor for more than three hours a day and more than eight chanting the Divine Office.

They also keep silence so strictly that wherever they are, even at work or some other situation, whatever it may be, they never speak without the permission of their superior. But despite this uniformity of life, where [human] nature finds no respite or relief in variety itself or in some change in austerities and labors, this never seems to pose any problems for these good monks. For them, the love of God renders all things sweet, and however heavy the cross they bear, they yet find it too light. One never hears them complain or sees them shirking their work: instead they hasten to it with extraordinary joy and delight, and they have for each other a truly brotherly love[107] and respect.

Among the novices you see a childlike obedience, even though most of the twelve or thirteen there at present are priests, and some more than fifty years old.[108] But in no way do they find this shameful, for it is in humiliations[109] that they

---

[107] *Charité*, but here, for once, it is better translated as love. But the love the brethren have for each other is that properly directed love of which Saint Augustine speaks in n. 105 above.

[108] This statement concerning the number, nature, and age of the novices appears on page 80 of the first (1671) edition and remains unchanged in the new edition of 1689.

[109] Humiliations is, effectively, a technical term in Rancé's vocabulary, and there is a long section devoted to it (or them) on pages 314–409 of the first volume of the first edition (1683) of Rancé's *De la sainteté et des devoirs de la vie monastique*. Further on humiliations, and the controversy between Rancé and Guillaume Le Roy, commendatory abbot of Hautfontaine (and, before the controversy, one of Rancé's friends), see François Vandenbroucke, "Humiliations volontaires? La pensée de l'abbé de Rancé," *Collectanea Cisterciensia* 27 (1965): 194–201 (English translation as "De Rancé on Deliberate Humiliations," *Cistercian Studies* 8 [1973]: 45–52), and Bell, *Understanding Rancé*, 125–26, 145–46, and 296–97.

find their glory, and all these holy men, who could appear in the world renowned and esteemed, have renounced all that the world finds most delightful. They find it sweeter to bury themselves in the wilderness and live in humility, and their love is given only to the most rigorous austerities.

But in no way are these timid and cowardly slaves led by a valiant captain! They are rather free and noble men who walk in the footsteps of their leader, who obey him with overwhelming love, and who, like him, always have their weapons at the ready to counter the attacks of demons. Indeed, they always see him at their head. Are they going to church? He is the first to enter and the last to leave. In the refectory, his austerity is greater than any, for he usually eats only one portion of his meal and inflicts on himself the harshest penances. Are they off to work? He chooses the hardest [tasks] and spares himself so little that in summer he leaves [his work] in just the same way as do his monks, drenched in sweat, to go into the church, where it is still very cold. There they all stay, and the water on their bodies soaks into the serge of their habits so much that they often return to work the next day in habits still wet with the sweat of the day before.

But apart from all the privations that Monsieur l'Abbé suffers with his monks, he has his own personal sufferings in the care that he takes in keeping watch on all they do. Not only does he himself go into all the places where they are working to see how they conduct themselves there, fearing that someone might fall into laxity without noticing it and let [his thoughts] go scattering about in exterior things, but he is also extraordinarily diligent in observing them at their manual labor. He watches those who act with too much fervor, and when he sees that they are working too hard at moving earth or carrying some burden, he has them leave aside their task and do some raking, or peel vegetables, or some other less heavy work. Thus, with his eyes always upon them, he inspires the least active and holds back those who have too much ardor.

But what he practises with regard to bodily exercises, he also observes with those of the spirit. For although he does not detect the slightest imperfection in his monks without immediately correcting it, he also has admirable discretion in not overburdening them with penances, for he believes that he would be equally guilty before God for being either too harsh or too lenient with them. Finally, having no other thought than to unite these holy souls by the bonds of charity, and to kindle in them more and more that divine fire that ever burns in his own heart, we see that he never forgets anything that may further increase their love for this Sovereign Beauty. And in this he feels no jealousy, but only wishes that the whole world would adore [that Beauty] with the same ardor with which he loves it himself.

There is a parlor[110] in the cloister where he sometimes speaks with his monks when they have some particular thing to say to him. I have noticed that on one of the walls he has had inscribed these beautiful words of Saint Augustine:

> *Retinebant nugae nugarum et vanitates vanitatum antiquae amicae meae.*[111]

And on the opposite wall:

> *Sero te amavi pulchritudo tam antiqua et tam nova, sero te amavi.*[112]

These words are there as a public monument to the religious sentiments that possess his soul. And in confessing that the vain amusements and foolish vanities of the world were the

---

[110] Building no. 19 on **Figure 1**, on the north side of the chapter room.

[111] Augustine, Conf 8.11.26; PL 32:761: "Trifles of trifles and vanities of vanities, my old friends, held me back." *Vanitates vanitatum* echoes Eccl 1:2 and 12:8.

[112] Augustine, Conf 10.27.38; PL 32:795: "Late did I love you, Beauty so ancient and so new, late did I love you!"

very links that once bound him to it, he now expresses his regret for having spent so long in neither knowing nor loving this eternal Beauty that, at one and the same time, is so ancient and yet so new.

On the rear wall of the same parlor one may also see inscribed these words:

In me sunt Deus vota tua.[113]

Here he reveals to God the present state of his soul, for God alone is ever the sole object of all his desires.

But all this, Madame, is no more than a sketch of the exterior things that can be seen in this happy solitude. If one could really see and describe what is inward and hidden in these solitaries, one would produce an incomparable painting, far more wonderful than anything I have offered here. What colors could we use to portray all that occurs in the depths of their souls, the never-failing fountain of that humility, respect, and submissiveness[114] that these religious have for their abbot? What brushstrokes could delineate the zeal and love Monsieur l'Abbé has for them? His constant vigilance of which I have just been speaking? His diligence in attending to all their needs while, at the same time, never being distracted by worldly concerns or by worrying about whether the revenues of his abbey are sufficient to sustain a community that is growing day by day?

Indeed, he thinks so little of these things that he regards them as a heavy burden and believes them to be even more burdensome than they are useless to monks who can live on so little and who should set their sights only on eternal goods. Indeed, I have heard it said that, for him, it would be his greatest joy if they possessed nothing at all and had not even a

---

[113] Ps 55:12: "In me, O God, are vows to you."
[114] Or "obedience" (*soûmission*).

building to live in. "In which case," he would say, "we would make little huts in these woods and around these lakes, just like the ancient solitaries of the Thebaid.[115] We would find enough to nourish us, and, being less rich in the good things of earth, we would work harder to acquire the good things of heaven." Nor did one ever speak of legal proceedings or lawsuits at the abbey. The procurator[116] of the house never has to concern himself with these troublesome requests. In the view of this holy abbot, it is so great an evil that he believes that there is nothing in the world that should involve any religious in such things. He said to me one day, "If circumstances should arise in which [by going to law] we could keep what belongs to us, or otherwise lose it unjustly, I do not believe that we should leave our cells and disturb the peace of our souls either to demand what belongs to us or to defend ourselves against those who want to seize our goods. Just as there is nothing so wicked as lawsuits, there is nothing one should not do to avoid them. As for me, I believe that if Scripture teaches us to give even our tunic to those who want to seize our cloak,[117] then this precept has been written especially for monks! Far from seeking to increase their revenues, they ought to abandon them to the violence of those trying to seize them rather than leave their solitude to fight them."

Thus he advises his monks never to enter into lawsuits, however just their case may be. "But if it is so important," he says, "that it seems impossible to put up with it, then go and find the person who wants to seize your possessions, and inform him charitably of the injustice he is doing to you and the evil he is doing to himself. But if, in the hardness of his heart,

---

[115] I.e., the Desert Fathers.

[116] The monk charged with the administration of the financial affairs of the abbey.

[117] Matt 5:40: "If anyone wants to sue you and take your coat, give him your cloak as well." See also Luke 6:29 for the parallel.

he will not listen to you, take your case to the judges whose business it is to uphold your rights, and after that, rest in peace and trouble yourself no more: whatever happens will only be what divine Providence[118] has decreed."

Such are the ideas of this incomparable man, who has no desire whatever to increase the domains of his abbey nor, under some specious pretext of upholding the rights of the poor, to dig out old documents and use them to impoverish widows and orphans through lawsuits and legal quibbles.

He is not content, however, merely to teach these things: he also puts them into practice. Some years ago an eminent nobleman acquired a piece of land in the area that required the payment of a small rent to the abbey of La Trappe. But since the contract had been made without the knowledge of Monsieur l'Abbé or his monks, there had been no attempt on their part to uphold their legal rights [to the rent]. Some time later [they became aware of this] and demanded from the nobleman the arrears that were due to them. He, however, produced his contract and showed them that he actually owed them nothing, for he had acquired his piece of land without (it seemed) any mention of rents due to the abbey. For the monks, this response was sufficient. They made no attempt to take the trouble of finding out how to make him pay. They continued to spend their days in silence and tranquility, wholly reconciled to their loss.

But then God himself spoke for them in the depths of the heart of this nobleman and made him aware that the simplicity of the monks' lives should not deprive them of what was due to them. As a consequence, and even though he did not believe that he was legally bound to become a new debtor to the monks, their conduct, and the odor of sanctity with which they perfumed the whole locality, led him to acknowledge the principle of the rent and pay the arrears due to them.

---

[118] See n. 50 above.

We see here how God blesses all good intentions, and we also see two excellent examples of that practice of charity that Saint Paul requires of all true Christians.[119] On the one hand, we have the monks who suffered the loss of their possessions patiently and without bitterness; on the other, we have the nobleman who did not pursue his own interests, but actually abandoned them rather than preferring them to that justice one should render to every person at all times. This story should be a good example to those who abuse the rights of prescription[120] that the Law has established only against unjust claims, and who take advantage of it to avoid paying what they know they justly owe.

But the charity of Monsieur l'Abbé and his monks does not extend only to abandoning their possessions and suffering those who have usurped them to enjoy them in peace. Since the only thing that can afflict them is the sinfulness of those who have seized their goods, they do all they can to save their souls. Some time ago, it happened that certain properties located near the abbey belonged to [the monks] by right of forfeit, and some individuals had seized them but until then had given no [legal] reasons for what they did. It would not, in fact, have taken much in the way of legal procedure to get back what was rightfully theirs, but, as I have said, they regard lawsuits and disputes as such dangerous evils that even the shadow of the smallest quarrel appals them. This, then, was their plan, as told to me by Monsieur l'Abbé: "We will send for the people who have taken the property, and we will show them that what they have done in seizing the land is unjust.

---

[119] See 1 Cor 13:4-8, and n. 105 above.

[120] *Prescription*—the same word in both French and English—refers to the method of acquiring an easement or right of use upon someone else's real property by regular and continual use for a specified length of time (usually a number of years) without the specific permission of the owner of that property.

But at the same time, since they have neither the will nor the power to divest themselves of it, we will give them the land as a gift and thereby do as much as we can to alleviate their conscience."

You can well imagine, Madame, that such disinterested religious never dream of acquiring new lands or instituting legal actions. Indeed, disdaining a prudence they consider all too worldly, they do not even put aside some of their revenues to provide for their needs in bad times. This is so contrary to their way of life that Monsieur l'Abbé does not believe they should save anything at all, and should it happen that the years are so fertile and so abundant that the poor have no need of their help, he has no desire to put aside anything while someone in need may turn up. He often says that Christian charity does not allow us to turn away our brother without furnishing what he needs, and that Scripture teaches us that we should not concern ourselves at all about tomorrow.[121]

It is because of this disinterest in and disdain for all earthly goods that these happy solitaries continually raise themselves up to heaven. Furthermore, when they enter this house [of La Trappe], it is like a tomb in which they are buried alive.[122] Their only goal is to rid themselves of this mortal body, and, with Saint Paul, they ask God unceasingly when the happy and blessed day will come that they will be delivered from it.[123] It is this desire that sustains them in the silence they keep so strictly. Days on which they have Conferences[124] are, for them, days of recreation, and when they are gathered round their

---

[121] Matt 6:34: "Do not therefore be worried about tomorrow, for tomorrow will have its own worries."

[122] See Bell, *Rancé*, 107–8, 215.

[123] See Rom 7:24: "Wretched man that I am! Who will deliver me from this body of death?" See also Rom 8:23.

[124] The nature, purposes, and conduct of the Conferences are set out in some detail below (from n. 276 onwards).

abbot at the end of some walkway or under the trees, they listen with inexpressible joy to the talks he gives them on the bliss of eternity, for he speaks only of holy things. They know nothing whatever of current events and what is happening in the world, and they have no interest in the quarrels of princes or the way the state is run. They are content to pray each day for the king and to supplicate heaven on his behalf while he governs the people whom God has entrusted to his care.[125] Indeed, unless the names have been changed in the prayers said in church, they do not even know that one pope has succeeded another. They are like travelers who no longer look back to the place they have left but whose eyes are ever fixed

---

[125] The king was Louis XIV. One of Rancé's biographers, Jacques Marsollier, archdeacon of Uzès and a professional historian, tells us that there were three libellous accusations levied against Rancé and his monastery: "The first was that the Virgin was not honored at La Trappe; the second was that hardly any Masses were said there; and the third was that there was no liking there either for the king or for the government, that [the abbey] harbored suspect persons, and that cabals against the State were hatched there" (Jacques Marsollier, *La vie de Dom Armand-Jean Le Bouthillier de Rancé, Abbé régulier et Réformateur du Monastère de la Trappe, de l'Étroite Observance de Cisteaux. Nouvelle Édition* [Paris: H. L. Guerin & L. F. Delatour, 1758], 2:127–28). All three accusations, says Marsollier, have been explained and shown to be manifestly false. How? Because the practices that Rancé established at La Trappe required that "six Masses were said every day: one of the Office of the Day, one of the Virgin, one for the Dead, a fourth for the king, one for the benefactors, and a sixth for the persecutors and enemies of the monastery" (Marsollier, *Vie de Rancé*, 2:127). And to this regimen the abbot added a further requirement that every day, before Vespers, there should be fifteen minutes of prayers for the king. This, says Marsollier, was done at the monastery "avec le plus d'exactitude" (Marsollier, *Vie de Rancé*, 2:127), and as far as he was concerned, the evidence of these six Masses and the royal prayers did away with all three of the calumnies we mentioned above. On the veneration of the Virgin at La Trappe, see n. 81 above.

on where they are going, and who achieve their goal in spirit before they have arrived there [in body].

It is a pleasure, Madame, to hear Monsieur l'Abbé speak of the bliss of the life to come. His words are like a devouring fire that sets aflame all who hear them. You may perhaps remember with what eloquence he expressed himself on worldly things while he was still at Court:[126] this cannot be compared with the force and power with which he speaks of the things of heaven, of the end of the world, of the blindness of those who prefer the joys of [earthly] life, so short and full of misery, to the delights of eternal felicity, of the bliss of the saints, of the blessed state of those who, here below, have a true love for God. He likens them to a mirror turned to the sun and says that the light of the reflected sun in the mirror dazzles the eyes. For a single soul filled with this love is so penetrated by

---

[126] The young Rancé had been interested in preaching from an early age. In 1643, when he was only sixteen, he wrote to his old tutor, Jean Favier (see n. 43 to the Introduction), that not only were his theological studies proceeding apace, but that he would like to begin preaching as soon as possible (Rancé, *Correspondance*, 1:65–66 [Letter 431100]). His public preaching began, in fact, three or four years later, in 1646 or 1647, when he preached at the convent of the Annonciades on the rue de la Couture Sainte-Catherine in Paris. Other sermons followed, including an Easter sermon to the male Discalced Carmelites in their house on the rue de Vaugirard. A great crowd had gathered to hear the twenty-year-old preacher, and if we may believe Dom Pierre Le Nain, who is not an impartial witness, his sermon was received with universal admiration (Pierre Le Nain, *La Vie du Révérend Père Dom Armand-Jean Le Boutillier de Rancé, abbé et réformateur de la Maison-Dieu Nôtre-Dame de la Trappe* [(Rouen): (n.p.), 1715], 1:11). The young Rancé was not unaware of his own abilities. On one occasion, when he met François de Harlay de Champvallon in Paris—he was a friend who, one day, would be archbishop of the city—Harlay de Champvallon asked Rancé what he was doing that day. "This morning," he replied, "I'll preach like an angel; this afternoon I'll hunt like a devil" (Gervaise, *Jugement critique*, 56–57).

Divinity that it seems already to be the same as God.[127] "And," he says, "just as the Philosophers' Golden Stone purifies all other metals in such a way as to turn them to gold as well, so, at the end of time, God will perfect and purify all things and make those he has chosen similar to him."

When anyone speaks to him of penitence[128] and the austerity of the life they live [at the abbey], he counts it as naught, and he believes that once monks have left the world and truly given themselves to God, they should count all the mortifications they can endure as a mere trifle. "We serve a Master," he says, "who has made himself nothing for us, who has stripped himself of the glory of his divinity to clothe himself in our misery.[129] We can truly imitate him only by making ourselves nothing. If we wish to share in the bliss of eternity, we must suffer for

---

[127] The key word here is "seems" (*semble*), for in orthodox Christian teaching the soul never actually becomes God: the creature never becomes the Creator. It may *seem* to do so, but it does not. Bernard himself makes this clear when he describes the fourth degree of love, the love of self for the sake of God, in the *De diligendo Deo*. Here, he says, the soul is truly united with God, and that union is similar to a drop of water being mixed with a quantity of wine: the water *seems* to lose itself in the color and taste of the wine. His other analogies are that of red-hot iron, which *seems* to have renounced its natural form and become one with fire, or that of air so flooded with sunlight that it *seems* to be not so much lit as light itself (Bernard, Dil 10.28; SBOp 3:143). In the words of William of Saint-Thierry, we do not become God (*Deus*), but "what God is" (*quod Deus est*): good in his goodness, wise in his wisdom, pure in his purity, and so on (see David N. Bell, *The Image and Likeness: The Augustinian Spirituality of William of Saint-Thierry*, CS 78 [Kalamazoo, MI: Cistercian Publications, 1984], Chap. 3 [89–124]). It is the restoration of the lost likeness.

[128] *Pénitence* in French can mean penitence, penance, or repentance, or all three at the same time.

[129] Phil 2:7.

him as he suffered for us, and in renouncing everything we consider important, we must even renounce our own will."[130]

Such, Madame, are the discourses of this amazing man, and the usual subjects of his conversation. What he says is accompanied by such an air of joy that it is easy to see how convinced he is in his soul of what he says and to see the pleasure he feels when he expresses outwardly the true sentiments of his heart, sentiments he tries to communicate to everyone.

Such holy thoughts and so great a detachment from all earthly things lead to a truly tranquil life and can only be followed by a glorious death. Since the time that Monsieur l'Abbé undertook the reform of this abbey[131] there have been only two deaths: one of a Brother Oblate, the other a professed monk. The former was a gentleman from Champagne who had given all his goods to the poor, following the example of his elder brother who had retired to the abbey of Perseigne at the time that Monsieur l'Abbé was serving his novitiate there.[132] The

---

[130] In Augustinian terms, the renunciation of self-will (*propre volonté*: Félibien's term) is the same as the renunciation of self-love, since love and will are, in essence, the same. See Augustine, De Trin 11.5; PL 42:988; 15.38; PL 42:1087; and 15.41; PL 42:1089. Thus the less we love ourselves, the more we can love God, and the more we love God, the less we wish to do our own will. In the end, our will is united with God's will, and we become, as Athenagoras of Athens put it, a musical instrument on which God plays (Athenagoras, Apol 7).

[131] That is to say, in the seven-year period from July 1664, when Rancé entered La Trappe as its regular abbot, and 1671, the date of the first edition of Félibien's *Description*. There is no change to this sentence in the new edition of 1689, though by that time it was certainly incorrect. In 1674 there was a sudden and dramatic increase in mortality at the abbey that occasioned much comment in the outside world. It was partly the result of the unhealthiness of the site, and partly the result of an inadequate diet, seriously lacking in protein. See further Krailsheimer, *Rancé*, chap. 5 (83–101), and Bell, *Understanding Rancé*, 109–10, 223–24.

[132] I.e., from June 1663 to June 1664.

younger brother went to Perseigne to find the older, and sometime later they both came to La Trappe, where they asked to be [admitted] as the least of the servants. The elder brother is still at the abbey and continues to live the sort of life that he and his brother had begun. The younger was the porter of the Outer Court and undertook all the most humiliating and demanding tasks. Monsieur l'Abbé had a little lodge built for him near the gate where he could make a fire and live a life somewhat less austere than that of the monks. Yet we may say that he surpassed them all in his austerities, living exactly the same life as the monks, continually occupying himself with [manual] labor and mortifying his flesh with exercises of his own devising. He was, in the monastery, like those stars one sees that appear to be smaller and less brilliant than the others, but that are actually that much higher in the heavens.

He used to dress like a layman in a simple brown habit with a knee-length coat[133] of the same [color] tied with a belt, a battered hat, and wooden clogs. For two years he suffered so much from the cold in winter and his body was so penetrated by it that he developed three ulcers on his left breast and two on one thigh. Since he had become extremely feeble, he could not shake off a minor intermittent fever, and [it was accompanied] by such great pain in every limb and such violent stomach cramps that he could not even move around [on his pallet] to change position. He suffered continually from asthma, and it was a great relief to him when, sometimes, he could turn

---

[133] The knee-length coat is a *juste-à-corps* (or *justaucorps*), which was worn by men in France in the second half of the seventeenth century and throughout the eighteenth. It was introduced into England as part of a three-piece ensemble with breeches and a long waistcoat, and was thus the ancestor of the modern three-piece suit. The *juste-à-corps* was often made of the most luxurious materials with magnificent embroidery, though this, naturally, was not the case with our oblate porter at La Trappe.

himself just a little, but this happened only rarely. Yet he endured all this pain with admirable patience, and instead of complaining loudly about his sufferings, he praised God for the grace he was bestowing upon him. If Monsieur l'Abbé encouraged him to take a little food and tried to sympathize with his sufferings, he maintained that he was still too happy. "There is not one of your monks," he would say to him, "who does not suffer a thousand times more than I." When his illness gave him a few moments of relief, he occupied himself with sewing on his bed and often with reading. He had only two books, which he read constantly: the Psalms with a commentary and *Le Chrétien intérieur*.[134] Someone advised him to read the *Ecclesiastical History*[135] for a change, but he returned the volume that had been given to him and took pleasure only in the other two, which, for him, were the usual nourishment of his soul.

One day, when Monsieur l'Abbé saw that he did not have long to live, he spoke to him of death. "My brother," he said, "you see that the time is drawing near when you must appear before God. Are you not afraid to present yourself before so awful a judge, who will demand from you an exact account of all your actions?" "My father," he replied, "I admit that when I look on my miserable condition, I find nothing there which should not fill me with dread. But when I consider the mercy of my God, I have such confidence in his goodness that even when I see hell open before me I shall pass over its flames and fear nothing."

---

[134] A very popular work by Jean de Bernières, sieur de Louvigny (1602–1659), edited posthumously by the Capuchin Louis-François d'Argentan (1615–1680). It was first published in 1660 with numerous later editions. There were two copies in the La Trappe library (see Bell, *Library*, 296–97 [A.43–A.44]).

[135] Probably the *Ecclesiastical History* of Eusebius of Caesarea, of which printed editions had been available in Latin from 1497 and in French translation from 1500.

Saint Augustine says that in God there are two types of mercy: one for heaven and eternity, which is concerned with eternal goods; the other for earth and this [earthly] life, which is concerned with temporal goods.[136] It would be presumptuous of those who have never served God but who, instead, have enjoyed the transitory goods of earth, to believe they are assured of sharing in eternal rewards. But for someone who is so far from pursuing worldly riches and an easy life that he has given all he possessed to the poor so as to be yet more poor than they, and who, illumined by the light of Faith, has never asked of God anything more than that mercy that is in heaven, such a one may certainly hope that God will not refuse him this grace.

Finally, after fifteen months of suffering, it was apparent that his strength was failing and he was given the last rites.[137] After this, all the monks prayed the prayer for the dying, and when the happy moment arrived—the moment this good brother had sought unceasingly—he gave up his soul to God in profound peace, leaving on his face the marks of his soul's joy. For I have heard it said by Monsieur l'Abbé, who told me the story of this death, that the brother's face, which was so emaciated by his austerities and his long illness, appeared after his death to be so beautiful that he did not tire of looking at it and did not wish to cover it. In this way the death of the saints, which is precious before God,[138] is also beautiful in the eyes of men. In this place, there is nothing about death that is in the least frightening either to those who suffer it or to those who witness it.

While this good brother was in his death agony, the monks who were assisting him had withdrawn to a corner of the room and were saying Vespers, and his elder brother was on his

---

[136] I have not yet found this passage in Augustine, if, indeed, it is Augustine.

[137] Lit. "given the Sacraments."

[138] Ps 115:15.

knees at the foot of the bed. Having seen him expire, he remained motionless and waited until the monks had finished their Office. He then said to them in a very low voice, "He passed away shortly after you began Vespers." Thus, in this death, he demonstrated as much faithfulness and submission to the commands of God as his brother had shown in the patience and perseverance [with which he faced] his illness.

The monk who died about four months later was one of six who had been living in the abbey before the arrival of Monsieur l'Abbé,[139] but he was the only one who had embraced the reform. His name was Dom Joseph Bernier, and he came from Mortagne.[140] He had made his profession at the abbey of La Trappe in 1641 when he was twenty, but later, being resolved to give up the easier lifestyle in which he had hitherto lived and embrace the strict observance of the Rule of Saint Benedict, he made his way to Perseigne on September 1, 1663, and began [a new] novitiate [in the Strict Observance]. Since the life he had led before this was hardly consistent with the demands of his [monastic] vows, from then on he labored to make satisfaction to God by harsh penances, so much so that from once being a source of scandal[141] he had now become an edifying example.

Some months before his death he begged Monsieur l'Abbé to grant him four requests. The first was to remove him from the altar so that he could no longer say Mass. The second was to put him at the end of the monks' procession[142] as if he were the least of them. The third was that he would be permitted to make a general confession in the presence of all his brothers. And the fourth was that after his death his body would simply be dumped by the side of the road.

---

[139] See n. 22 above.

[140] See Dubois, *Histoire*, 103.

[141] Lit. "stumbling-block (*pierre de scandale*)," quoting 1 Pet 2:7.

[142] I.e., the processions to and from the church: see *Règlemens*, 24 (III.9).

Description of the Abbey of La Trappe (1689)   103

He continually pleaded with Monsieur l'Abbé, who still put off granting any of his requests until the novices who were there at that time would have made their profession. But God himself chose the type of ordeal through which he wanted him to reach the perfection of penitence, for he struck him down with a severe sickness in which he developed a gangrenous ulcer on part of his thigh, which was extremely uncomfortable and painful. And since it was often necessary to cut away the living flesh, he suffered terribly for the space of fifteen days. Yet he endured his sickness and all the operations with an admirable patience. When he came to the end of his days, he received the last rites and was laid on ashes in accordance with the custom of the Order.[143] Then, while the monks were in the church, he said "Jesus" three times and gave up his soul to God. But when the monk who was at his side heard him say these words in a much stronger voice than usual, he thought that he was recovering, and that he had uttered these words in a spasm of pain. Thus it was that he died without anyone being aware of it.[144]

It must be said, Madame, that in the art of loving God there are secrets that are known only to the saints, just as in other arts there are secrets known only to those who practice them and that other men and women cannot appreciate. In the past this good father had lived a wholly worldly life under the [monastic] habit of devotion, and while he did so, he never thought of punishing his body with some degrading torment, and there was nothing that seemed to him more odious than to be condemned to sufferings that he himself had asked to have imposed. But after he had embraced the Reform [of

---

[143] See *Règlemens*, 86 (XII.12). This is in accordance with the regulation in the *Ecclesiastica officia* 94.1; Choisselet/Vernet, 268–69. The monk dying on straw and ashes is a recurring theme in the *Relations de la vie et de la mort de quelques religieux de l'abbaye de La Trappe*.

[144] According to Dubois, *Histoire*, 103, he died on September 15, 1670.

Monsieur l'Abbé], even though he chastised his body with severe penances, even though he seemed to have purified himself by the water of his abundant tears[145] and all the harsh austerities he had suffered to sanctify his soul, he did not believe that he could sufficiently avenge himself upon himself [for his former way of life]. He regarded himself with such horror that he wished to make himself as nothing, and in depriving himself of a grave—an honor of which he considered himself unworthy as a consequence of the irregularity of his former life—he sought to efface his name from human memory.

These sentiments of a penitent soul are the sacrifices that God regards with joy. But just as he showed Abraham how constant he had been in his obedience and in the disposition of his heart,[146] so Monsieur l'Abbé (who, among his monks, is the voice of God and the interpreter of his will) showed by his prudent conduct in not wholly complying with the desires of this monk how inconceivable (as I have just said) are the secrets of loving and serving God. But while one cannot understand them, one should nevertheless wonder at them without being in any way surprised that one person appears to be so cruel to himself and another so merciful. Nor should one judge lightly those events, so extraordinary and so surprising, that are manifested in the life and death of the saints.[147]

If it were possible, Madame, to have a record of everything that happens at La Trappe, what Christians would find com-

---

[145] See Ps 6:6.

[146] See Gen 26:5; Heb 11:17-19. God tested Abraham by demanding that he sacrifice his only son, Isaac, and then, after angelic intervention and Isaac's happy deliverance, promised the latter that through his descendants all the nations of the earth would be blessed, "because Abraham obeyed me, and kept my instructions, commands, statutes, and laws."

[147] The next fifty or so pages of the new edition of 1689, containing the two *relations* of the edifying deaths of two monks of La Trappe (pages 113–65), do not appear in the first (1671) edition.

forting is to see, every day, what contentment is to be found in bearing a yoke as easy as the yoke of Jesus Christ.[148] They would see one of the great miracles of the love of God, namely, that for the monks, the joy that comes from [living their lives] in penitence is equal to the suffering that comes from penitence itself. Indeed, this joy takes the place of all other joys, for the vows taken by these anchorites are followed by a perseverance in virtue that lasts until the final moment of their lives.[149]

This is just what we can see in the story of what happened [at La Trappe] after the deaths of the two religious of whom I have just been speaking. The third, who was received at La Trappe in 1659,[150] was twenty-three years old. From his youth

---

[148] See Matt 11:30.

[149] In this last sentence, Félibien is referring specifically to the Augustinian doctrine of the final perseverance (*perseverantia finalis*) of the saints, as set out in his *De dono perseverantiae* and *De correptione et gratia*. Its basis is Matt 24:13: "Whoever shall persevere to the end shall be saved." It means, in essence, that God may make sufficient grace available to certain human beings—namely, those predestined to receive it—so that they, in cooperation with this grace, and only in cooperation with this grace, may remain in a state of grace until the end of their lives. Cardinal Newman explained it thus: "The gift of perseverance consists in an ever watchful superintendence of us, on the part of our All-Merciful Lord, removing temptations which He sees will be fatal to us, succouring us at those times when we are in particular peril, whether from our negligence or other cause, and ordering the course of our life so, that we may die when we are in a state of grace" (John Henry Newman, *Discourses Addressed to Mixed Congregations* [London: Longman, Brown, Green, and Longmans, 1849], 137 [from Discourse VII "Perseverance in Grace"]).

[150] This is the date given by Félibien, but it cannot be correct. In 1659 Rancé had only just begun to see clearly the road that would lead him to La Trappe. The identity of this monk is unclear, but he may have been Frère Guillaume Monceaux, born at Chemiré-le-Gaudin in the diocese of Le Mans, who was professed at La Trappe on September 4, 1675, though Dubois, *Histoire*, 129, no. 41, has his age as twenty-two, not twenty-three. Félibien tells us later that the brother of whom he is writing died in the sixth year of his profession,

onwards he had shown no interest in the care taken with his education, and he was so unruly that there were grounds for thinking there was something very dangerous in conduct as wretched as his.

But if, like Saint Paul, he was the scourge of good people before his conversion, he was soon afterwards their consolation when he changed his way of life to one wholly opposite to that which he lived formerly. To him we can apply the words spoken by Jesus Christ in reference to Saint Paul: "I shall make him feel how much he should suffer for the glory of my name."[151] For following the example of this great apostle, he showed after his conversion what effects grace could have on a heart penetrated by divine love. Until then this good brother had lived without either the knowledge or fear of God: the world and its vanities were the only things he cared about. But even as he was thinking only of earthly things, a heavenly grace forestalled him. He knew God. His sins[152] filled him with horror. And from that moment he made the resolution to do penance for them.

How many are there who, nourished on the bread of tears,[153] can be compared to Saint Paul because they suffered great things for Jesus Christ? But we need not look far back in the past. La Trappe itself provides us with models of virtue that can touch our hearts, raise them up to God, and incite us to do penance with this good brother if we, like him, have lived our lives in iniquity.

---

which is exactly the case with Frère Guillaume, who died on May 24, 1681.

[151] Acts 9:16.

[152] *Crimes*, which does not here mean "crimes" but "sins." It is a common usage among seventeenth-century French spiritual writers. Much nonsense has been written about Rancé's saying that "religious congregations are gangs of criminals" (*De la sainteté et des devoirs de la vie monastique* [1683], 1:392): he simply means that they are collections of sinners, not that they are wanted by the French police.

[153] Ps 79:6.

How swift would be our conversion, and what happiness would follow, if we could hear the reproaches he would make against himself. He called his body a rebellious and insolent creature, a savage and untameable beast, a viper seeking to kill the soul that gave him life. He reproached himself unceasingly for his wayward youth, from his eyes he shed torrents of tears to wash away all the stains of his sins, and he dedicated himself to doing the sort of penance on which he had resolved. "What difference does it make," he would say, "if my health is destroyed and my body weakened? It will still be strong enough to enslave my soul and make it rebel against the will of God."

Consumed by these ideas, he took the monastic habit. But where? At La Trappe, for he knew that the life there was truly austere, and that the example of the monks would provide him with great support. He also hoped that he would find it easier to persevere under the guidance of Monsieur l'Abbé, of whom he had earlier heard tell. Nor was he mistaken in his expectations, for from the time he entered the abbey, Monsieur l'Abbé never ceased to provide him with the spiritual food he needed and to lead him in the way of eternity, and, for his part, this good brother made every effort to make himself a worthy disciple of such a good master. In so doing he followed the example of those holy anchorites of old who were convinced that we should never rely too much on ourselves or on our holiest resolutions. He was afraid he would fall into the misfortune of those who are too healthy and who are brought low when they put too much trust in their own strength. He was only too well aware that the time of temptation and the time of illness were equally unpredictable, for he well knew that every man and woman is subject to the corruption of sin and death.

As soon as he found himself among the monks of La Trappe, he sought every way of doing penance that would be acceptable to God and move him to be merciful. He began by being so assiduous and vigilant in his conduct that from his conversion to his death he was never heard to say a useless word and never seen to do any action that was not absolutely necessary. His continual restraint showed clearly that his sins were ever before his eyes and that God's [impending] Judgment made a strong impression on his spirit. It was easy to see how scrupulous was his conscience in this matter and how he examined his motives and his conduct at every moment, for he had recourse to Monsieur l'Abbé if he found himself in the least difficulty. He listened in profound humility to the advice and instructions that he gave him with regard to his conduct, and he never failed to put them into practice on every necessary occasion. It may even be said of him that he was as faithful in following [the advice of Monsieur l'Abbé] as if he knew it had been given to him by God himself through the mouth of his prophets. One day Monsieur l'Abbé came to him to examine his conscience, and what he confessed to him then is a clear indication that he never felt a greater joy and peace than when he could reveal to him [the secrets of] his heart. "When I think of the Judgments of God," he said, "I am terribly afraid. But when I pray, I feel myself overwhelmed by the greatness of his divine majesty, and that fills me with comfort."

From then on Monsieur l'Abbé knew well that this good brother had the best intentions, and to encourage him to continue as he had begun, he said to him, "My brother, be vigilant and scrupulous in God's service, and think often on what you have become in the religious life and why you left the world. Remember that God is always ready to reward the faithfulness of his servant. He has even promised it in these words: 'Happy is the servant whom the Lord finds awake and watching when he comes. Truly I say to you that he will set him over all his possessions.'[154] Listen to the promise that God

---

[154] Luke 12:43-44.

makes to you, my brother, for it stems from his love. And if you never cease being faithful to him, there is no doubt that he will be merciful to you."

So strongly did this discourse of Monsieur l'Abbé touch this good brother that he redoubled his austerities, but whatever he did, he still thought it was less than what he owed to God for his misspent past. When he spoke of eternity, it was only with fear and trembling, and with new torrents of tears. He implored the help of the Holy Virgin. He prayed to Jesus Christ, [asking him] to apply to him the merits of his passion to make up what was lacking in his own sufferings. "My God," he would say, "do not spare this sinner who is more worthy of your justice than your mercy. Have me wash away the enormity of my sins[155] in the waters of penitence, and deign to apply to me the merits of your passion so that my sins should not be an obstacle to your love."

And then, whether God wished to give this good brother some indications of his love, or whether he wanted him to realize that the most arduous and onerous labors become easy as soon as one undertakes them [only] with the intention of pleasing him, it was immediately apparent that this good brother was now at peace and unconcerned with regard to God's Judgments. And his joy became so great that he lived amid his sufferings in perfect contentment.

The monks, as well as Monsieur l'Abbé, obviously noticed the abrupt change. They were naturally surprised and could not help wondering at it. But the good brother, who had hitherto distrusted himself and refused to believe himself capable of ever moving God to mercy by his true penitence, continued his austerities without showing the least anxiety about the future as he had done earlier. And while he sought every opportunity for humiliation,[156] he never ceased to live

---

[155] *Crimes*: see n. 152 above.
[156] See n. 109 above.

in peace and always seemed to be as content as if he were certain of enjoying everlasting bliss after his death.

For more than a year he was seen to be laid low with such excruciating rheumatism that, without the special help of grace, it would have been impossible for him to have borne it as he did. But during the course of his sickness he was so steadfast that it astonished even the strongest monks. I admit that a similar degree of steadfastness can come from the care that Monsieur l'Abbé takes for the spiritual health of those who are sick. Since he has the true knowledge of salvation,[157] he never allows his monks to mitigate [their austerities] while they are ill. He has them keep the Rule as far as is possible, and practice mortification and humility until the last moment of their lives. But these holy anchorites, inspired by the spirit of God, call on his name as soon as they feel their sufferings increase, and very often they forestall Monsieur l'Abbé, who is [always] ready to speak to them to encourage them in this holy action. This is just what happened in the case of this brother. He would be heard to say, "Lord, you are all powerful and I am nothing but weakness. You are the master and I am only your slave. Do not spare me in these short-lived sufferings so that I may deserve eternal joy." This good brother was always to be found with this attitude, but it was particularly apparent six weeks before his death, when his patience was such that he provided every monk of La Trappe with a fine example to follow.

Apart from his terrible rheumatism he also contracted a respiratory problem[158] that was so severe that one would have said he was ready to yield up his soul at any moment. Yet never for a moment did his excessive sufferings stop him from ap-

---

[157] See Luke 1:77: "science de salut" = *scientia salutis*.

[158] Lit. "an oppression of the chest." I suspect that the problem was tuberculosis, exacerbated by spittoons in the church (see n. 202 below) and dirty handkerchiefs in the dormitory (see *Règlemens*, 13–14 [II.5]).

plying himself to his prayers with as much fervor as if he had just begun them. One never saw him lose heart in his holy works, nor did he ever mitigate his devout exercises. He lived each day as if he were convinced it would be the last day of his life. And it was during these [last] six weeks that he had many opportunities of giving Monsieur l'Abbé clear indications of his piety.

As soon as he felt the acute onset of his pains he lifted up his heart to God, blessed his justice, and asked that he might be subject to his will. Then, looking at Monsieur l'Abbé, he said to him, "I am blessed, my father, in what you have encouraged me to suffer for the love of God. I take such comfort in seeing myself in this condition that I never ask him to relieve my sufferings nor to lighten his hand. I ask only that I submit to his holy will and that I may be always ready to obey you in all that you wish me to do."

When Monsieur l'Abbé saw that the good brother was approaching his end, he watched over him continually and spared no pains to support this penitent soul in the holy state in which he found himself. On one of those days he asked him if he did not feel himself becoming weaker, and this good brother, prostrated by the severity of his sufferings, replied that he did indeed find himself profoundly feeble. But as soon as Monsieur l'Abbé made him understand that he was not speaking of his body but his heart, he replied, "Alas, my father, as for my heart, that is in the hands of God. I hope for all his clemency and I await death as true happiness. I tell you, my father (he continued) that my soul is filled with holy consolation, for God is ever present to my spirit save for those brief intervals when I am drowsy because of my insomnia. Life is wholly unimportant to me: if God grants my wish, he will take me from this world. But I would not have him hear my pleas if they are contrary to his will."

For a long time this good brother discussed the state of his soul with Monsieur l'Abbé, but after that he hardly spoke to him at all, for he developed an inflammation of the tongue that prevented him from speaking—or, more accurately, that allowed him to express himself only with great difficulty. Yet the way in which he conducted himself was so moving and so full of devotion that it clearly revealed the depths of his soul.

Monsieur l'Abbé, whose vigilance allowed him to use every moment profitably, immediately prepared him to receive the [last] sacraments. They then took him into the church, where he received the holy Viaticum[159] with his brothers, and then Extreme Unction.

Shortly afterwards he became very weak, and Monsieur l'Abbé, who never left him for a moment, did all that he could to sustain him in the confidence God had given him. And to assure himself of what had occurred in the heart of this good brother, he asked him if he still had a firm hope [in what was to come]. And even though this good monk was so close to death, he replied steadfastly, "My father, I hope in our Lord without any doubts. He has given me the time to do penance, and he will be merciful to me." Then, raising his eyes to heaven, he uttered a few prayers and rendered up his spirit while thanking God for the grace he had given him in letting him die in the hands of Monsieur l'Abbé, in the presence of his brothers, and on ashes and straw.[160]

This good brother was in the sixth year of his profession when God fulfilled his desires by [granting him] a happy end. As he had wished to die in the same way as the monks who had died before him, God granted him this grace, together with a profound peace. Such were the fruits of the penance he had done following the example of his brothers.

---

[159] The *viaticum*, "provisions for the journey," is the term used for the Eucharist administered, with or without the Anointing of the Sick, to people close to death or on their deathbed. If the dying person cannot take any solid food, the *viaticum* may be administered in wine alone.

[160] See n. 143 above.

Most Christians do not make early preparation by true penitence [to meet] the justice of God. They give themselves to God only after they have sickened of the pleasures of the world, but they come worn out with these same pleasures. The life they lead is too spineless and relaxed to expiate the sins they have committed, and all they can expect is everlasting punishment.

There are others living in the world who are indifferent to their salvation, but when they are close to death they have no scruples about offering to God the last few moments of their lives. But should they not be ashamed to offer so little to God, who has given them so much? Should they not be afraid that he will refuse them and cast them out forever from his divine presence?

To avoid this misfortune, which is the greatest of all misfortunes, let us all begin to do penance as soon as possible, and if we are not so happy as to follow [completely the way of life of] these anchorites of La Trappe, let each of us do what God demands of us according to our situation: let us love him; let us be humble and submissive to his Church. And if we have to live in the world, let us flee its detestable principles, which can only cause our fall and render us unworthy of eternal salvation.

I see, Madame, that I have unintentionally wandered from my subject and have not satisfied your desire to know the details of the life and death of the monks of La Trappe. If it pleased God, Madame, that everyone had a spirit like yours, it would only be necessary to recount the actions of these holy anchorites, and then, by reading them, each person would understand (as do you) that these narratives[161] are not so much to satisfy the curiosity of the faithful as to edify them.

---

[161] *Relations*: the same word as in the *Relations de la vie et de la mort de quelques religieux de l'abbaye de La Trappe,* which first began to appear in 1677.

Those who are full of the spirit of the world would be amazed to see virtuous people renounce all earthly honors to pass their lives in obedience. But if God touched their hearts with a particular grace, they would then understand that his elect can be nothing but humble. Far from following that accursed angel[162] whose pride brought about his fall, they could never rest while they did not see themselves practising profound humility among the monks of La Trappe. It is there that they would find subjects worthy of admiration. Neither [noble] birth nor advanced age, nor even a former life in a position of authority, prevents them from subjecting themselves entirely to the Reverend Father Abbot. In his hands they are as soft wax that he can form and mold as he pleases. How could it be otherwise, since he himself is the first to provide them with examples of perfect humility?

It was just this humility that, long ago, led Saint Gregory to flee from Rome and hide away in a cave so as to avoid being pope.[163] It was this same virtue that led Saint Peter Celestine, the pope and founder of the Celestines, to resign willingly from his pontificate and step down from the throne of Saint Peter to return to his beloved solitude.[164] And, as we have seen

---

[162] I.e., Lucifer.

[163] The tale is told in the Golden Legend: *Jacobus de Voragine. The Golden Legend: Readings on the Saints. Volume I*, trans. William G. Ryan (Princeton: Princeton University Press, 1993), 173. Gregory hid himself for three days in the cave, but to no avail. A beam of light shone down from heaven onto the place where he was hidden, and a certain hermit saw angels ascending and descending on the beam. This led those who were seeking Gregory to his hideout, and he was brought back to Rome and, against his will, duly enthroned as pope.

[164] Pietro Angelerio or Pietro da Morrone was elected pope on July 5, 1294, at the age of seventy-nine, taking the name Celestine V. In 1244 he had founded the order that was subsequently named after him—the Celestines—who were, essentially, a stricter branch of the Benedictines. The order became extinct in the course of the eighteenth century but still existed at the time Félibien was writing. Celestine was hopelessly unprepared and unequipped for the papacy, and he

in our own days, it is just the same [virtue] that has led an abbot to resign his abbatial dignity and spend the rest of his life at La Trappe in prayer and mortification.[165]

He was then seventy-seven and had been twelve years in his former abbey, but after [his term as abbot had expired and] a successor had been elected, he wrote to the Reverend Father Abbot of La Trappe begging him to receive him into his house to do penance. In his letters to Monsieur l'Abbé he made it quite clear that he was proceeding in this matter with all possible freedom, and that far from finding any difficulty in relinquishing the authority he had had over his own monks, he fervently wished to see himself among the novices at La Trappe so as to practice the obedience they observed at the abbey. "To be able to end my days," he said, "in this state of humility would be the greatest happiness possible, and I hope, Monsieur, that you will not refuse me the grace I ask of you: to be utterly subject to your [spiritual] direction, for I value the condition of being a servant of Jesus Christ more than being an abbot in my own monastery."

These ideas came from a heart wholly imbued with divine love, and it did not take the Reverend Father Abbot of La Trappe long to recognize the source of this living water[166] that gushed forth with such force and vehemence. He therefore wrote a favorable reply to the abbot, who left [his own abbey]

---

resigned after five months as pope on December 13, 1294. He wished only to return to his eremitical solitude, but his successor, Boniface VIII, fearing that he would be the focus of anti-Boniface sentiment, had him imprisoned in a castle in southern Italy. There he died on May 19, 1296, after ten months of captivity.

[165] The abbot was Jacques Minguet, formerly abbot of the Strict Observance monastery of Châtillon-en-Lorraine. An account of his life and death, which follows closely that of Félibien, appears in the *Relation de la vie et de la mort de quelques religieux de l'abbaye de La Trappe. Nouvelle édition* (Paris: G. Despez, 1755), 1:145–49. See also Dubois, *Rancé*, 1:532–37.

[166] John 7:38.

at once and made his way to La Trappe. But what did he not do after he had been received? Prayer, fasting, and [manual] labor became his occupation, and so strict was he in practising them that he could hardly eat or sleep without regretting the time he spent in these necessities of life. Although he had always lived according to the Strict Observance and had been exemplary in the regularity of his life and as a source of edification, [when he came to La Trappe] he kept all the austerity [of the Rule] without any dispensation and found therein his nourishment. He was never seen to take a moment's rest after Matins,[167] and even when the [rest of the] community had left the church at midnight, he remained there in prayer until Prime, which was normally said at half-past five. After that he busied himself throughout the day with his allocated work, something he continued to do right up to the onset of his illness. But the most admirable thing about him was the way in which his advanced age never stopped him from humiliating himself by accusing himself in Chapter[168] with all the meekness and simplicity of a novice. If it happened that someone proclaimed him[169] and reproved him for his faults (which, in such

---

[167] Félibien has already told us that Matins usually began at 2 a.m. and could last up to four and a half hours, but that included the Little Office of the Virgin and half an hour's meditation. If there were time, the monks could retire to their cells for a brief rest before Prime at 5:30 a.m. See n. 83 above.

[168] The reference here is to the Chapter of Faults, at which all those monks who had made the vow of stability accused themselves publicly of any infringements of the Rule of Saint Benedict, of the customs of the abbey, and/or of any specific rulings of the abbot: see n. 294 (and following) below. The Chapter of Faults took place in the chapter room.

[169] In this case, a monk is accused or "proclaimed" by one of his brothers of one or more of the infringements mentioned in n. 168 above. In his Regulations, Rancé refers to proclamation as "the foundation and nerve center of the whole regular discipline of a house" (*Règlemens*, 45 [VII.3]) and spends some time in setting out exactly

a pious person, were very light and very rare), he followed the example of Jesus Christ and maintained a humble silence,[170] and, then, deeply regretting that he had offended, he would say within himself, "What's this, my God? You never have to justify your innocence, so shall I, a miserable sinner, have the nerve to excuse my faults? No! I only ask you to forgive them, and my heart, pervaded by the deepest sorrow, awaits all your mercy."

When our abbot had been living at La Trappe for five years in the way I have just described, he found himself deprived of his sight. But this deadly blow in no way affected his virtuous strength, for he endured his loss not only by resigning himself perfectly to the will of God, but even by recognizing his loss as a grace and a result of God's mercy. "What right have I," he would say, "to complain of my problems? Are not both health and sickness works of the Lord? And who am I to dare penetrate his intentions? May your name be blessed, O my God, and may your will be done. If the insects that crawl about the earth can contribute to your glory, are not human beings capable of glorifying you in whatever condition they may be? I will therefore suffer, Lord, as much as it pleases you, and if you will permit my sufferings to efface my sins, [I will suffer] most joyfully!"

Since he was now unable to celebrate the holy sacrifice of the Mass, he was seen to spend his days in continual prayer, ever singing the praises of his Lord, and communicating at the holy table three times a week and on whatever feast days were held. It could be said that from that time on he awaited death

---

why and how it is to be done. "We do not proclaim on the basis of suspicions, doubts, or hearsay; we state only the faults we know, from having seen or heard them, and [that we do] as briefly as possible" (*Règlemens*, 46 [VII.4]). Rancé is here following the *Ecclesiastica officia*, 70.68 (Choisselet/Vernet, 206–7).

[170] See Matt 27:13-14.

at every moment and that the only thing he found grievous about it was that it was too slow in coming. When it was time for him to rest, he would lie on his pallet as if he were sleeping in the tomb, and however much he prepared himself for a holy death, one could see that he was always afraid that he would not have the strength to undergo its sufferings, for he was well aware that a death that comes in the midst of torments is always accompanied by the hope of a joyful eternity.

It happened [at this time] that the Reverend Father Abbot of La Trappe fell ill,[171] and even though the monks had all the confidence in him that one ought to have in a superior, the prior had to take over the running of the monastery. The latter then came to visit our abbot [Minguet] and asked him if there was anything he needed. "Alas!" he replied, "the only thing I need is to be humbled, and I beg you never to spare me!" After this reply, can we doubt that he was ever watchful to avoid the misfortune of those foolish virgins spoken of in Scripture?[172] His heart was aflame with divine love and was ever bound to the one who filled it, and it is there that we find the holy oil he sought to preserve in himself, lest his lamp—I mean his soul—might cease to burn with divine love at the very moment the Son of God would come to take him to himself.

But in loving the Son in this way, he lacked nothing in honoring his holy Mother with a remarkable devotion.[173] Apart from the usual fasts, he also fasted every Saturday, the day

---

[171] This was in the spring of 1680: see Dubois, *Rancé*, 1:597–98.

[172] The reference is to the parable of the Wise and Foolish Virgins in Matt 25:1-13. Of the ten virgins, five were wise and brought extra oil for their lamps in case the coming of the Bridegroom was delayed. The five foolish virgins brought only their lamps with whatever oil was in them, but while they were waiting, their lamps went out. When they returned later, presumably after having got more oil, they found the door to the wedding feast shut in their faces.

[173] For a study of the veneration of the Virgin at La Trappe, see Bell, "Armand-Jean de Rancé (1626–1700) and the Mother of God," *passim*; and for Dom Minguet, see especially p. 47.

devoted to the worship[174] of the Holy Virgin, and since he knew that the Queen of the Angels is the refuge of sinners, the consolation of the afflicted, and the succor of the faithful, he addressed to her unceasingly his desire that, through her intercession, he might share in the merits of the blood of Jesus Christ poured out on the cross. He had such an exalted idea of his Savior's passion that whatever penance he did, even flagellating himself[175] three times a week, he still maintained that he lived without virtue, without penitence, and without mortification. He begged the Reverend Father Abbot of La Trappe to join his prayers with his own so that God might give him a pure, contrite, and humbled heart,[176] for he was convinced that his works were of hardly any consequence when compared with the sufferings endured by Jesus Christ in the course of his life [on earth].

God, who knows all, was fully aware of the faithfulness of his servant, and since he saw that the time was approaching when, through his Providence,[177] he had determined to reward him, he had him feel the effects of his mercy. This was when his illness resulted in the loss of all his natural faculties under the burden of his advanced age and the austerities he had practiced for almost eight years. His [last] illness began towards Holy Week in 1681,[178] after he had kept Lent with a rigor that defies description.

---

[174] *Culte*, which does not here mean "cult" in the usual modern sense.

[175] Lit. "taking a rigorous discipline." A "discipline," in both French and English, is a term for the scourge used by some members of certain religious orders for self-flagellation. Its popularity in the Middle Ages and in early modern times owed much to its encouragement by Saint Peter Damian, a very odd man.

[176] See Ps 50:12, 19.

[177] See n. 50 above.

[178] In 1681, Palm Sunday, the beginning of Holy Week, was March 30. Easter Sunday was April 6. Dom Minguet died on Palm Sunday: see n. 185 below.

When the Reverend Father Abbot saw him in this condition, he ordered him to give up for a little while the extraordinary austerity of his life, and it was at this moment that our invalid had a wonderful opportunity to exercise his humility by prompt obedience. But in no time at all he was earnestly entreating the Father Abbot to allow him to finish his course as he had begun it, making the case that it was God's will and that vegetables were quite enough to ease and nourish him.[179] Thus his request was granted, and, despite the severity of his sufferings, he continued to live as he had lived before, namely, in strictest penance.

This admirable and holy conduct brought home to me the danger to which we are exposed by our attachment to life [in this world]. Invalids who wish passionately for the restoration of their health might perhaps be excused from having so natural a desire if, indeed, they could avoid death. But since one of these days death must come to us all, what is there to be gained in trying so desperately to delay it? Sooner is better, especially when one is so well prepared [for death] as these devout solitaries of La Trappe.

As a result of the Father Abbot's assiduous care for his sick monks, almost every one of them entrusts his spirit into his hands, and in so doing they find their greatest comfort. They feel that the presence of a man so filled with virtue gives to their own souls new strength to lift themselves up to God.

Just one day before his death, the abbot of whom we have been speaking displayed clear evidence of the goodness he had experienced by being guided by Monsieur l'Abbé. As soon

---

[179] Dom Minguet was in the infirmary (that is clear from what follows), and those in the infirmary who were seriously ill or who had continual fevers were permitted certain sorts of red meat—beef, veal, or mutton—though never more than once a day, "according to the ancient Statutes of the Order": see *Règlemens*, 79 (XI.4). Dom Minguet refuses this mitigation.

as he saw him in the infirmary he was filled with joy and cried out, "My Father, I know well that the hour of my death is upon me, and that the goodness of God is infinite, for he has done me the favor of [allowing me] to die in the faith of the All-Holy Trinity, in your arms, and in union with all my brethren. Pray for me, so that I may experience yet again the effects of his mercy and go to him filled with consolation."

After this he revealed to him the whole state of his soul, making him understand how sorry he was for living a life so little worthy of a Christian. He told him again of his great fear of the Judgments of God and the pains of purgatory, but that this did not stop him from trusting in his mercy inasmuch as he believed its effects would be communicated to him through the prayers of the Church.[180] It was this that led him to view death as the beginning of a truly happy life and as the end of all his sufferings.

These good sentiments were accompanied by so vibrant a faith that one could clearly see that he was moved by the spirit of God and that truth was to be found in his words. He then finished by saying to the Father Abbot that he had a special favor to ask of him, and the latter, with great affection, immediately said to him, "What is it that can I do for you, my brother?" "My Father," he replied, "I am about to give an account before God of all that I have done, and his mercy imbues me with confidence, but the memory of my transgressions terrifies me. I have need of prayer, and I know that his infinite goodness can, in an instant, deliver me from the multitude of sins that I have committed in the course of my life. That is why I beseech you that, apart from the usual prayers, one of the

---

[180] It was (and is) the traditional teaching of the Roman Catholic Church that the prayers of the faithful could assist souls in purgatory, so that they might enter more swiftly into the eternal joys of Paradise.

monks should say Mass for me on each day of the trental."[181] "It shall be so," replied Monsieur l'Abbé. "On that matter you can put your mind at rest." The joy he found in this pleasing reply moved him to tears, and all who were in the infirmary heard him thank Monsieur l'Abbé for granting his request, and then, raising his heart to God, he cried aloud, "There is nothing more now that I desire, and I may die in peace. *Nunc dimmittis servum tuum, Domine.*"[182]

As he had prepared himself [for death] during the day by a general examination of his whole life, so, as soon as night came, he indicated that he wished to make his confession, and realizing that he had no time to lose, he begged Monsieur l'Abbé to hear him and help him make a good end.[183] After he

---

[181] The trental—*tricénaire* in French—is a series of thirty Requiem Masses said on thirty consecutive days for the repose of the soul of someone departed. Its legendary origin is to be found in the sixth century when the deceased mother of Gregory the Great appeared to him while he was saying Mass and asked him for his help in releasing her from her purgatorial pains. She specified that she needed a series of thirty Masses, which he dutifully celebrated, and she then appeared again to him, as a being now of heavenly beauty, and he had the gratification of seeing her escorted into Paradise by an angel. See further Gwenfair W. Adams, *Visions in Late Medieval England: Lay Spirituality and Sacred Glimpses of the Hidden Worlds of Faith* (Leiden: Brill, 2007), 23–24.

[182] Luke 2:29: "Lord, now lettest thou thy servant depart [in peace]," the first line of the Song of Simeon.

[183] *Faire une bon fin.* In the seventeenth century, "making a good end" was the proper, public, and dramatic conclusion to living (in theory) a good life. Ideally, one would die in one's bed, surrounded by family and friends, after making one's confession, being given absolution, and receiving communion and extreme unction. There would then come the spectacle of the funeral cortege, the somber tolling of the bell, the Requiem Mass, and the final interment. It was all a public act, carried out according to established customs and the appropriate rites. Things changed in the eighteenth century, but that is not here our concern. For a riveting account, see John McManners,

had confessed, he then asked permission (as he himself had resolved) to receive the holy Viaticum[184] the following morning, which was Palm Sunday.[185] The prior, who was there present, said that because he was now so very feeble the sacraments would be brought to him in the infirmary, but this suggestion had such an impact on him that, with absolute determination, he said assuredly and loudly that he had quite enough strength to go into the church, and that he would rather drag himself there by his hands than fail in his duty.

His zeal and fervor were too great to refuse him the complete freedom to do as he wanted, and he seemed [then] to be just as content as if the passage from life to death were no more than a few steps, easy and pleasant, which would take him whither God was calling him.

Scarcely had the bell rung for three o'clock in the morning than he raised himself up and, for the last time, prepared himself to receive his Creator,[186] as worthily as possible. It took him until four o'clock to make his acts of contrition, love, and humility, and I can truly say that there was no more edifying sight than the person of this good monk in his holy disposition. Furthermore, those who were at his side to comfort him were no less edified than astonished to see him making his way to church with as light a step as that of a healthy young man. They were delighted and amazed when he heard almost the entire Mass on his knees with an attention equal to his piety. And finally, they were unable to conceive that he was actually at the very end of his life when his face was enlivened with a beautiful light brought about by his rapturous love for God.

Death and the Enlightenment: Changing Attitudes to Death among Christians and Unbelievers in Eighteenth-Century France (Oxford: Clarendon Press, 1981).

[184] See n. 159 above.
[185] March 30, 1681: see n. 178 above.
[186] I.e., in the Eucharist.

It was then that he gave thanks [to God] for all his goodness, and especially that it had been his will to come and visit his servant one final time. There can be little doubt that in his last moments he repeated the prayer he had been accustomed to say since he lost his sight. This is how it went:

> My God, if I do not have the joy of seeing you with my bodily eyes, give me so deep a faith that you may always be present to my spirit. Grant that I may be so moved by the blessings you bestow on me at every moment that I may never cease to love you. And purify my soul so that it may have an everlasting memory of all the good things you have done for me.

Oh, what desire and what delight to taste in this way the sweetness of God, to be nourished by God alone, to search in solitude for God alone! What bliss must follow a life lived as our abbot lived it! No sooner had he made his act of thanksgiving in the church than God drew him to himself, and just when he was ready to return to the infirmary his soul left his body, worn out with old age and beaten down by that continual penitence that led him to Jesus Christ.

Who would not wish to have lived eighty-four years as he did, and to have spent almost eight of them at La Trappe, so as to make at the last an end as joyful as his? I swear that almost the whole of his life was no more than a succession of austerities, and that in his own abbey, just as at La Trappe, he had conducted himself with the strictest [monastic] regularity. But we must surely agree that all this is as nothing when compared with the everlasting pains [of hell], and that we shall be forever happy if the experience leads us to understand how sweet it is to die when one has known how to live well.

I do not know, Madame, when I should finish [my account of La Trappe] if I were to write down all that I have learned and all that I have seen in this holy solitude, where the monks are detached from all worldly things: how they treat them with disdain, and with what courage they labor to please heaven. One day we were talking with Monsieur l'Abbé in the library:[187] there were three of us with him at the time, one of whom was one of his particular friends, a very devout canon of Paris and very learned Doctor of the Sorbonne. We were speaking of contempt for the things of the world when one of us said to him that he knew of some people who found it scandalous that at the end of his letters he signed himself (so they said) as a bishop, simply writing "Armand-Jean, abbot of La Trappe,"[188] and that he still made use of the seal and coat of arms of the house.

"These people," he replied, "are obviously deceiving themselves. Even though I might sign [my letters] in the way they criticize, they should not find anything to blame in that since many others have done the same thing. Indeed, there are a number of letters of Saint Bernard in which he signs himself simply "Bernard, abbot of Clairvaux." But even so, ever since I became a monk I have never written my name without putting F[189] in front of it. And as for the seal we use, it is that of the abbey, and it displays two chevrons that were part of the escutcheon of the founder,[190] as you can see on the vaulting of our church. I would indeed be unhappy (he continued) if, after giving up the position and all the comforts I had in the world to make my salvation more secure, I should still preserve so slight a desire for honor and endanger my salvation by attaching myself to such a ridiculous and vain trifle. But it is inevitable that the Evil One always interferes in our affairs."

[187] Building no. 14 in **Figure 1**. See further Bell, *Library*, 36–37.
[188] See Rancé, *Correspondance*, 1:44-45.
[189] More accurately, fr. for *frère*, "Brother": see Rancé, *Correspondance*, 1:45.
[190] The arms of the lords of the Perche were argent three chevrons gules, i.e., three red chevrons (like upside-down V's) on a white or silver background. It was a design shared by a number of noble families in Europe.

On that note he then told us how someone had tried to turn away a [prospective] monk (who is presently still a novice) by sending him a forged letter saying that when he came to La Trappe he should not fail to bring with him the appropriate sum of money [as his monastic dowry].[191] It is true that those who had written the letter had signed it "Dom Pierre, abbot of La Trappe," and that it was not difficult for those who received it to see that it was forged, not only from the handwriting and the wrong name, but also from its self-seeking contents that were so alien to the spirit of the house.[192] But these little misadventures, and anything similar that the Devil can raise up against Monsieur l'Abbé, are so far beneath him that he simply ignores them. "We let the world say what it will," he said; "we pay it no heed whether it blames us or praises us. Nothing it can do or say holds us back for a mo-

---

[191] The requirement that a monk (often) or a nun (almost always) should bring a dowry when entering a religious house was common from the early Middle Ages onwards. There was always opposition to it, not least because it could be regarded as a form of simony (the buying and selling of ecclesiastical office), but it was too entrenched a custom to be eliminated. Mabillon was certainly opposed to it. "It is most shameful," he wrote, "that men who have once and for all relinquished everything, and who are sufficiently endowed, should demand a dowry from those whom Christ has called to himself" (Jean Mabillon, *Annales Ordinis S. Benedicti Occidentalium Monachorum Patriarchae. Tomus Quintus* [Paris: C. Robustel, 1713], 315). But despite the fulminations of canon lawyers, not least canon lawyers who were popes, the system continued, and, as George Coulton has said, "If the dowry system is less often mentioned in papal pronouncements during the last generations of the Middle Ages, and less commented upon by official visitors, this is not because the strict disciplinarians had won, but rather because they had lost heart" (George G. Coulton, *Five Centuries of Religion. Volume III. Getting and Spending* [Cambridge: Cambridge University Press, 1936], 238). Coulton's whole account (pages 232–40) may be recommended.

[192] No dowry was demanded at La Trappe. One could not buy one's way into Rancé's abbey.

ment, and we press on straight to God, the one and only object we should have in our view and the only voice to which we should respond."

It seems to me, Madame, that in the operations of grace we see a great similarity to what happens in the workings of nature. When one plants an acorn, and the damp warmth of the earth causes it to decompose, this little seed (which is like the soul) strips itself of the rough and coarse [skin] that surrounds it and immediately puts forth roots deep into the earth, roots that come forth only after it has established a firm foundation for the great tree that, in time, it will become. It then grows with such vigor that it surpasses both in strength and height all the other trees of the forest and, despite gales and storms, raises its head to heaven. Can we not say that grace has achieved something similar in the person of this holy abbot? He left the world to plant himself, to bury himself,[193] in the midst of this desert after he had stripped himself of all that he had inherited, all his benefices and responsibilities, all his numerous servants and horses, all the honors he possessed, and whatever he could claim by virtue of his birth, his merits, his mind, and his great knowledge. After this, I say, after he had left all the comforts and pleasures of life in the world, he began to steal away from the eyes of men and, humbling himself before God, to put forth the deep roots of that virtue that cannot be forever hidden and that, raising itself as far up to heaven as it abases itself by its humility, put him above all the storms and tempests that the malice of the devil might stir up against him.

We see that of all trees, those that grow in places with the worst soil and the most stones are the most hardy and provide wood the least susceptible to rotting. In the same way we can say that it is in the midst of austerities and mortifications that

---

[193] The verb is *enterrer*, which means both to plant and to bury. Félibien is continuing his metaphor of the oak tree but also referring to the monastery as a tomb (see n. 122).

the virtue of these holy monks is strengthened and put to the test by all the attacks of the world and of hell.

It has been some time, Madame, since I had the honor of speaking with you, yet I dare not promise myself that you will have no more questions after what I have told you. For one comes across so many remarkable things and so many notable events in the lives of these solitaries that it is difficult to write them all down, yet they make these lives truly wonderful.

When we read the stories of the solitaries of old, we often find that we do not have sufficient faith [to believe] all that we are told. And why? Because the places where they practised their austerities were so far away, because of the number of centuries that have elapsed since that time, and because of the eloquence of those who knew how to put their actions in a good light. But [with regard to La Trappe], Madame, there is nothing in what I have written to you that cannot be witnessed by everyone. These wonders are taking place in our own day, here in the middle of France, and, indeed, my fear should not be that people will think I am exaggerating, but that they will blame me for not giving a sufficiently detailed account of everything that could be said.

I am,

MADAME,

Your most humble and most obedient servant,
**** [194]

NOTICE

It is possible to learn everything about life at La Trappe from the description we have just presented, and it would be unnecessary to write more had not certain important people

---

[194] I.e., four asterisks (two in the 1671 edition). As we saw in the Introduction, the book was published anonymously.

indicated their eagerness to see the Constitutions of the Order, just as they were made at its very beginning. For that reason, we have added the following account, in which you will find set forth the tiniest details of the life that is lived there.

An Historical Account of the Constitutions of the Abbey of Our Lady of La Trappe[195]

No one can be called a true Christian if the grace of baptism does not inspire them to lead an onerous life. And even if it seems that those who walk in the world have the privilege of going to heaven by a less strict route than that taken by solitaries, there is no doubt that they are obliged in just the same way as these solitaries to find their nourishment in the cross and in opprobrium,[196] and to season their food with the bitterness of perpetual penitence.[197] It follows, therefore, that those who content themselves with merely admiring these Constitutions without practicing the rules of the Christian faith should tremble, and they should know that they are on the path that leads to perdition if they do not have the courage to enter upon the narrow[198] way that leads to salvation, and to live in the world without being attached to the pleasures of the world, whose maxims are so very different from those of La Trappe.

---

[195] The nature, origin, and authority of these Constitutions are discussed in the Introduction to this volume.

[196] Félibien uses the plural *opprobres*, and he means a mixture of shame in the eyes of the world, infamy, insults, injuries, and misunderstanding. He is echoing Lam 3:30, *saturabitur opprobriis*, which he quotes (in Latin) in the margin of page 178.

[197] Or penance: see n. 128 above. Félibien here quotes a variant of Lam 3:19 in the margin of page 178: *Memorare paupertatis meae, absinthii et fellis*, "Remember my poverty, the wormwood and the gall."

[198] Félibien is echoing Matt 7:13-14, but the word for narrow—*étroite*—also alludes to the way of the Strict Observance.

The monks of this house normally get up at two o'clock in the morning to chant Matins.[199] They are so punctual that one sees great uniformity in all their actions, and never, for any reason at all, does one see them anticipate the sound of the bell for rising, even though there may be very little time between the strokes sounded.[200] If the service is rushed, the prior, subprior, and cantor must do penance,[201] for the order of the service is an infallible means of preserving one's zeal for the Divine Office.

They observe such great restraint in choir that they are not even allowed to yawn, nor to lean on the edges of their seats, nor to greet anyone other than the Reverend Father Abbot. If, however, they should meet a bishop there, or some other

---

[199] This is also stated in the 1671 *Constitutions*, 1. The 1690 *Règlemens* are more complicated: the monks rise at midnight on feast days, at 1 a.m. on Sundays, holy days of obligation, and the solemn anniversaries of the dead in November and January, and at 2 a.m. on all other days (*Règlemens*, 1–2 [I.1]).

[200] The *Constitutions*, 2, state that the time between the two strokes of the dormitory bell for Matins should be very brief so as to allow no occasion for laziness (no snooze time, in other words). By the time of the *Règlemens*, there is no space at all between the two strokes (*Règlemens*, 2 [I.1]). What is happening here is that the monks were required to rise at the first stroke of the bell and be ready to proceed into the church at the second. But since the interval between the two strokes was so short, one might be tempted to anticipate the first stroke and rise before it had actually sounded in order to be ready.

[201] *Constitutions*, 3; *Règlemens*, 3 (I.1). To understand why the service might be rushed, it must be remembered that when the Psalms were chanted at La Trappe, there was a lengthy pause between each verse or part verse, and according to the *Constitutions* and the *Règlemens*, the pauses were to be observed meticulously (*exactement*) (*Constitutions*, 3; *Règlemens*, 3 [I.1]). The pause could be as long as it took to recite a *Pater noster*, perhaps thirty seconds. It must sometimes have been tempting to shorten the pauses.

person of note, they may make a modest bow, but they may not speak to them without permission.²⁰²

These devout anchorites are almost always uncovered²⁰³ in the church, and the same is true when they go there to make their own private prayers.²⁰⁴ They never go to the Service straight after work, but first make a short recollection, fearing that they may be prey to some inattentiveness.

Frequent prayer, order in church, and silence throughout the whole house are three things that they observe scrupulously, and one can say that the way in which [the priests] moderate their voices when they are saying their holy Mass is as admirable as it is surprising.²⁰⁵ It is true that these regulations relate specifically to the monks of La Trappe, but they also teach Christians that when they are in church they should never affect questionable personal idiosyncrasies of ostentation and hypocrisy, nor show questionable negligence by a lack of devotion or impiety. These same regulations also teach us that we should never abandon the God whom we adore to grovel

---

²⁰² *Constitutions*, 4; *Règlemens*, 3 (I.2). Both the Constitutions and the Regulations add that in choir, the monks must spit only in the spittoons, which were to be kept as clean as possible, and that from time to time the sacristan was to put lime in them. See also n. 158 above.

²⁰³ I.e., with their cowls down and their heads bare. Both the Constitutions and the Regulations provide further details as to precisely when the monks are to cover and uncover.

²⁰⁴ *Constitutions*, 6: "We pray as often as we can, whether in the church or in our cells, at any hour, [for prayer] is the only way to obtain from God the faithfulness and disposition necessary for our [monastic] state." See also *Règlemens*, 3 (I.2), which states that prayer is the most effective way to obtain from God the faithfulness we need in our vocation, and to advance in perfection.

²⁰⁵ This is explained more clearly in the Constitutions and Regulations: the priests should so moderate their voices when saying their private Masses that one never intrudes on the other (*Constitutions*, 8–9; *Règlemens*, 4 [I.2]). This, in turn, is taken directly from the *Ecclesiastica officia* 59.24; Choisselet/Vernet, 182–83.

before some created thing. It is shameful to break off our adoration of the living God to adore the vain idols of [worldly] greatness and beauty.

If the restraint[206] of these monks and their way of greeting others serve as lessons for all the faithful, the latter are no less instructed by the way in which they adorn the church. The vestments are made only from simple fabric or some [plain] woven stuff or wool, with a fringe of woven stuff mixed with silk, and without gold or silver.[207] Only the sacred vessels may be of silver.[208] This simplicity of ornamentation does not prevent one from seeing everywhere that great propriety that is a mark of the reverence one has for God. It is this same propriety that teaches those who enter La Trappe that the richest ornament is a pure heart full of divine love.

[*The Dormitory*][209]

It is not only in the church that the monks of La Trappe show great reserve. When they move about in the dormitory they do so with a gravity and modesty that condemns the levity of worldly people, and they never enter each other's cells without permission for any reason whatever.[210] Neither do they ever leave the doors of the dormitory open,[211] and those who are

---

[206] *Modestie*, which here means restraint, self-control, modesty, and simplicity.

[207] *Constitutions*, 7; *Règlemens*, 5 (I.3).

[208] *Constitutions*, 8; *Règlemens*, 5 (I.3), naming the chalice, the ciborium, the monstrance, the vessel for the holy oil, and (in the *Règlemens* alone) the patens. This is taken from the *Exordium parvum*, XVII; Waddell, *Texts*, 257, 438.

[209] The subtitles appear in the margins of the 1689 edition of Félibien's *Description*.

[210] *Constitutions*, 9, 10; *Règlemens*, 12 (II.3). The *Règlemens* make an exception for the infirmarian and the brother who is in charge of the wardrobe (*vestiaire*).

[211] *Constitutions*, 11, adds "nor the others," namely, the doors of the cells.

not occupied with any particular task must stay there and keep to their cells. The doors [of the cells] may be opened by the superiors to see if those within are employing their time usefully.[212]

When one knocks on the door of one of the brothers, he comes to open it straightaway, without making [the person] wait and without paying any attention to what is going on outside.[213] How clearly this shows us that laziness and overweening curiosity[214] are blameworthy [vices] in every type of person.

The beds that one finds in this room consist of a few[215] wooden planks resting on trestles, covered with a prickly[216] straw mattress six inches thick[217] at best, with a straw bolster at the head. But can I tell you—alas!—how little used are [these beds]? No. But may those who think only of rest and repose come to learn from these models of virtue to be truly penitent. May they, like them, be ever on guard. May they work for their salvation without respite, lest the common enemy surprise them and come upon them like a roaring lion to devour them.[218]

[The Refectory[219]]

And if they look only for an abundance of the most delicious dishes when they enter the refectory of these good monks, they will see what little it actually takes to feed a person. They will

---

[212] *Constitutions*, 10.
[213] *Constitutions*, 12–13; *Règlemens*, 11 (II.1).
[214] See n. 71. *Curiosité* is always bad.
[215] Two, according to *Règlemens*, 12 (II.4).
[216] *Piquée*: see n. 104 above.
[217] Félibien and the *Constitutions*, 13–14, say half a foot in thickness (*un demi-pied*); the *Règlemens*, 12 (II.4), say "two or three fingers at most," which is considerably thinner.
[218] 1 Pet 5:8.
[219] Building no. 26 on **Figure 1**.

also know how to be polite and courteous[220] in all that they do. Let them consider the countenances of these good fathers as they sit at table with downcast eyes, yet not leaning over [their food] too much.[221] They all seem to be acquainted with the decorum practised by well-bred people, and when necessity requires them to use the knife set before them, they use it so carefully that one is surprised to see them cut the bread in perfectly smooth slices, without seeming to make any particular choice [of where to cut], and eating whatever they are served without mixing one dish with another, which is no more than gluttony.[222] This abominable vice is wholly unknown among them, for very often they make do with bread alone, and at all times they avoid wine unless some pressing debility forces them to make use of it, and even then they dilute it with a large quantity of water.[223]

On fast days required by the Order, they have for their collation[224] a little fruit and four ounces of bread, and great care is taken to see that they do not have more than this, for they are meticulous in ensuring that the amount they receive is absolutely accurate.[225] On fast days specified by the Church,

---

[220] "Polite and courteous" renders the French *honnête*, which can mean honest, but here means polite, seemly, decent, becoming, civil, well bred, or courteous.

[221] Félibien says that they do not lean over too much. The Constitutions and Regulations add "over what they are eating" (*Constitutions*, 15; *Règlemens*, 15 [III.2]).

[222] For this whole sentence, see *Constitutions*, 16–17; *Règlemens*, 16 (III.2). For "no more than gluttony," the Constitutions have "no more than gluttony and vulgarity [*malpropreté*]," and the Regulations "no more than voluptuousness [*sensualité*] and vulgarity."

[223] See n. 68 above. The *Constitutions*, 19, also mention that what little wine was given was diluted with much water.

[224] See n. 95 above.

[225] According to the *Constitutions*, 17, the bread is to be carefully weighed every time, for it can too easily become six or eight ounces without noticing it.

they are served neither milk products[226] nor butter at dinner, and for collation they make do with two ounces of bread and no fruit at all.[227]

Except during Paschaltide[228] they observe the Wednesday and Friday fasts throughout the whole year, never violating the Rule and never receiving any dispensation, and apart from those [they also observe] the fast days required by the Church or the extraordinary [fasts] demanded by the Order that may occur in the same week, though on occasion some important feast may occur on those days, which obliges them to dispense [with fasting].[229] And apart from all these fast days both of the Order and the Church, for the whole of Advent they abstain from butter, milk products,[230] and cheese.[231]

On other days, their portion is often salad and butter, and their normal fare consists of vegetables, peas, beans, milk products, rice, oatmeal, and gruel,[232] but never fish or eggs.[233]

---

[226] *Laitage*, which is defined in the *Reglemens*, 20 (III.6), as gruel (*bouillie*), or a porridge (*gruau*) of oats or barley.

[227] The same amounts of bread also appear in the Constitutions (17–18), but by the time of the Regulations, the amounts have been reduced to two ounces on fast days of the Order and one ounce on fast days of the Church (*Règlemens*, 23 [III.7]).

[228] The fifty-day period from Easter Sunday to the Sunday of Pentecost.

[229] *Constitutions*, 18–19.

[230] See n. 226 above.

[231] *Constitutions*, 19; *Règlemens*, 21 (III.6).

[232] Quite how much difference there was—if any—between the tastes of milk products (see n. 226), oatmeal (*gruau*), and gruel (*bouillie*), is difficult to say. But we may certainly call it a bland diet.

[233] The *Constitutions*, 20, add (correctly) root vegetables to the list of the usual foodstuffs. The *Règlemens*, 19 (III.6), defines these as carrots, beets, potatoes, and turnips. Félibien's word for potatoes—*tartouffes*—is rare and colloquial. The more literary form is *tartaufles*, though that was also regarded as rather common. It does not mean truffles, as it has occasionally been translated. Potatoes first appeared in France at the end of the sixteenth century.

Of all the dishes I have just mentioned, only two are ever served at any meal, to which may be added a little fruit.[234] Even on days of [monastic] profession, First Mass,[235] or some major feast, whatever it may be, they are not given anything out of the ordinary.[236]

They do not know what intemperance is, for from the moment they are at table, they never manifest any eagerness to drink, however much they may need to. They also avoid [doing] anything idiosyncratic, such as starting their meal with fruit, cheese, or some other thing that is intended to be eaten at the end.[237] There is among them such a deep spiritual accord[238] that one would take them for angels rather than men.

When the kitchen servers[239] have brought everything necessary into the refectory, they themselves sit down at table to begin their own meal, which they finish after the first course. When necessary, they very often help the cook, and, if it is judged to be appropriate, they even do the cooking. This, however, does not apply to novices, who never act as kitchen servers and who are not permitted to speak to the lay brothers.

---

[234] *Constitutions*, 20–21.

[235] I.e., by a newly ordained priest, which is usually a Solemn High Mass.

[236] *Constitutions*, 21; *Règlemens*, 23 (III.8).

[237] *Constitutions*, 16, 20; *Règlemens*, 16 (III.2).

[238] "Deep spiritual accord" translates Félibien's *égalité d'âme*, literally "equality of soul."

[239] The kitchen servers, who changed each week (they normally entered upon their duties on Sunday after Lauds), ensured that everything was ready for the brethren to wash their hands before dinner and supper, served the meals, washed the dishes, swept up the kitchen, prepared wood for the fire the next day, and did other such tasks. On Saturday, the last day of their weekly service, they also performed the *mandatum*, or foot washing, the regulations for which appear in the *Règlemens*, 35–36 (V.14). The first server washed the feet of the brethren, beginning with the abbot; the second dried them with the towels he had prepared. See further *Constitutions*, 21–22, and the *Ecclesiastica officia*, 77; Choisselet/Vernet, 228–31.

He who does the serving and he who is served bow to each other, and they do the same again when the dishes are cleared away.²⁴⁰ The cook makes nothing that remotely resembles tasty treats.²⁴¹ He dresses the vegetables with only a little butter or with nothing at all, and he never ever uses any spices.²⁴²

This prohibition against using anything that can be called spicy is a salutary precaution for [preserving bodily] purity.²⁴³ It presupposes the distrust that good Christians should have with regard to their [natural] powers, for from them arises an enemy who can be overcome only by fleeing from any contest with him.

One never speaks in the kitchen, but only at the doorway, and only the refectorian,²⁴⁴ the brother in charge of the guests, the sacristan, and the kitchen server²⁴⁵ are permitted to enter.²⁴⁶

---

²⁴⁰ *Constitutions*, 22; *Règlemens*, 18 (III.4). See *Ecclesiastica officia*, 76.30; Choisselet/Vernet, 226–27.

²⁴¹ *Patisserie*, literally "confectionary." See *Constitutions*, 22; *Règlemens*, 20 (III.6).

²⁴² *Constitutions*, 22.

²⁴³ At the basis of this idea is the theory of the four humors, which goes back to Hippocrates and Galen. The details need not concern us, but in Félibien's time it was thought that spices would heat up the blood, and overheated blood would give rise to sexual desires and sexual dreams. Cassian devoted an entire Conference to the problem of nocturnal emissions: see *John Cassian: The Conferences*, trans./annot. Boniface Ramsey, Ancient Christian Writers 57 (Mahwah, NJ: Newman Press, 1997), 757–82.

²⁴⁴ The refectorian was in charge of everything concerning the refectory: tables, benches, napkins, jugs, bowls, plates, cutlery, food, drink, hand washing, and anything else that might need attention. It was a position of considerable responsibility.

²⁴⁵ *Kitchen server* is here in the singular, though there were normally two.

²⁴⁶ *Constitutions*, 23; *Règlemens*, 97 (XIV.8). The *Règlemens* add the cellarer and the infirmarian to the list of those permitted entrance. The kitchen is Building no. 27 on **Figure 1**.

[*The Warming Room*[247]]

On entering the warming room, one sees a table where each person, if he wishes, may go to read, either sitting or standing.[248] But if anyone moves closer to the fire he must always remain standing, except at the time of the Conferences.[249] One's posture should be proper and decent: one should not pull up one's habit, save by the smallest amount,[250] and one should not slide one's feet forward [toward the flames] too much. Nor may any [brother] take off his shoes or slippers.[251] Everyone keeps strict silence while warming himself,[252] and no one is allowed to have a book in his hands during his time there.

[The Cloisters[253]]

It is not only by the fire that one is forbidden to speak, but also in the cloisters,[254] and no outsider may be brought into

---

[247] Building no. 24 on **Figure 1**.

[248] This table at which one may read makes no appearance in the Constitutions or Regulations and would appear to conflict with Félibien's own statement that one cannot have a book in one's hands while in the warming room. Both the Constitutions and the Regulations state simply that one never reads near the fire (*Constitutions*, 24; *Règlemens*, 25 [IV]).

[249] *Constitutions*, 24; *Règlemens*, 25 (IV). The regulations for the Conferences appear below.

[250] *Règlemens*, 25 (IV): "Habits are not to be raised more than a little above the ankle."

[251] Shoes (*souliers*) were worn indoors during the daytime; slippers (*pantoufles*) were worn only at night. At work, the monks wore *sabots*, or wooden clogs.

[252] *Constitutions*, 24, speaks of *grand silence*; *Règlemens*, 25 (IV) of *un perpétuel silence*.

[253] The vertical rectangle marked *Cloître*, immediately to the left of the west end of the church, in **Figure 1**. Félibien's twenty-one lines for this section stand in marked contrast to the eleven pages in the *Règlemens*.

[254] *Constitutions*, 26, *un très-exact silence*; *Règlemens*, 30 (V.4), *un perpétuel silence*.

them without the permission of the superior. Every time one brother meets another, he should uncover his head and greet him with a bow. They do the same when greeting the abbots of the Order if they come across them [in the cloister], but in the case of the Father Abbot, they stop and turn towards him with a deep bow, using the whole body.[255] They do the same thing in the case of the Father Immediate of the house.[256]

[Manual Labor]

The obligation to take part in manual labor means that the spirit in which it is carried out is one of the most edifying things one sees at La Trappe, for no one ever begins [his work] without interior recollection, and the careful way in which these solitaries go about their work makes it clear that God rules all their actions.

As soon as the bell[257] rings for manual labor, all the monks and novices make their way to the parlor,[258] including the cellarer and other obedientiaries, the kitchen servers, and the brother who is responsible for the garden, in order to speak with whoever allocates the work to be done. After this, the monks take off their outer habit, which is called a cowl, and the novices [remove] their capes, each with as much modesty

---

[255] *Constitutions*, 26. In the *Règlemens*, this section on greetings appears towards the end under "Some Regulations and General Practices," which we discussed in the Introduction: *Règlemens*, 95–96 (XIV.6).

[256] The Father Immediate of an abbey is the abbot (or, in rare cases, the prior) of the motherhouse of the abbey. Today, after the re-foundation of La Trappe in the nineteenth century (after the French Revolution), the Father Immediate of La Trappe is the abbot of Cîteaux; in Rancé's time it was the abbot of Clairvaux. In 1671 the abbot of Clairvaux was Pierre III Henry, with whom Rancé was well acquainted. By 1689 it was Pierre IV Bouchu.

[257] By 1690, the bell has become a *tablette*, a wooden board beaten with a mallet: *Règlemens*, 63 (X.1).

[258] Building no. 19 on **Figure 1**.

and decency as they can, and they never appear without a hood[259] or scapular[260] on their head.

Every day they work for at least three hours:[261] an hour and a half in the morning and the same after dinner, and more if they are able, bearing in mind that one who does not work does not deserve to eat.[262] In this way, the monks create a garden for themselves that should provide them with all that they need to eat,[263] and while they are working there they greet no one, not even their superior.[264]

The brother in charge of the garden or the brother who allocates the work may speak or make signs to those who are busy with manual labor, but the monks themselves maintain a strict silence, and if any one of them has a pressing need to break that silence, he must speak to the brother in charge,[265]

---

[259] *Chaperon*, which was rather like a poncho with a hood attached to it. It was worn over the cowl.

[260] The scapular is a piece of cloth worn over the shoulders, hanging down in front and behind, with a hood attached. The Rule of Saint Benedict, chap. 55, requires it to be worn when monks are engaged in manual labor.

[261] *Constitutions*, 28; *Règlemens*, 64 (X.3).

[262] 2 Thess 3:10. See n. 99 above.

[263] Lit. "which should be their subsistence." This section is considerably expanded in the *Constitutions*, 28–31. The *Règlemens*, 65 (X.4), states that "they work their garden themselves, which should be their source of sustenance and the basis of their life, in imitation of our fathers."

[264] *Constitutions*, 31. The regulations in the *Règlemens*, 68–69 (X.8), are more complex: if the abbot is at work, wearing the scapular, he is not acknowledged with the usual bow. If he is wearing the cowl, he is acknowledged, and the same is true if he is with guests, even if he is wearing the scapular. And if he should come over to a particular brother to examine his work, he is acknowledged with a bow by that brother.

[265] Félibien uses the word *président*, which the *Constitutions*, 30, renders as "the one in charge there" (*celuy qui y préside*).

Description of the Abbey of La Trappe (1689) 141

and do so in a very low voice a short distance from where the others [are working].²⁶⁶ Special care is taken to interrupt the work of any brother who is applying himself to his task with too much zeal,²⁶⁷ but no one may leave a task he has begun in order to do other things without permission. They are sometimes permitted to leave their manual labor [to attend to other matters], but in such cases, they return to what [they left off] as soon as they have finished the task for which they left it.²⁶⁸

One never sees the monks complain, either when they find their work difficult or when they are unable to complete it. They are always calm and composed²⁶⁹ and make every effort to succeed in what they do.

If they are allowed to choose a particular task, it will almost certainly be the most mortifying,²⁷⁰ in which case they must be ready for everything they may have to face. Furthermore, if any brother, even the most junior in the house, should ask something of another, the latter must be quick to do what he asks, provided it does not conflict with the intentions of the superior.²⁷¹

The occupation of the monks is not confined only to work in the garden. They also busy themselves with everything there is to be done in the monastery, without ever being less

---

²⁶⁶ *Constitutions*, 29–30; *Règlemens*, 67–68 (X.7).

²⁶⁷ Félibien has dealt with this problem earlier. It also echoes *Règlemens*, 67 (X.6), which states that such overzealousness is usually the effect of some hidden vanity or a passing mood or a natural inclination. It is not the Holy Spirit, who never acts imprudently and always does things in just measure.

²⁶⁸ *Constitutions*, 30; *Règlemens*, 67 (X.6).

²⁶⁹ "Calm and composed" translates Félibien's *tranquilles*.

²⁷⁰ *Constitutions*, 31; *Règlemens*, 66 (X.5).

²⁷¹ *Constitutions*, 31–32.

assiduous in [the celebration of the Divine] Office or their devotional exercises.[272]

They sweep up, they do the laundry, they clean out the stables, they help the lay brothers, and if any of them has a particular trade, they put it to work as the superior wills. They can also work outside the monastic enclosure, provided that they do so without communicating with seculars, or with the [hired] domestic servants of La Trappe, who never work with the monks—and such domestic servants should be dispensed with as far as is possible.[273]

Should we not find in all Christians this same spirit and this same eagerness for manual work? Who could excuse someone who does not work from the penance that God has imposed, to eat their bread in the sweat of their brow?[274] Was it not Jesus Christ who, for thirty years, worked for his living, and did not Saint Paul make tents?[275]

[The Conference]

The monks of La Trappe may not converse together, and there is no communication between them, any more than with any monks outside [the monastery walls].[276] Three times a

---

[272] *Constitutions*, 32; *Règlemens*, 64–65 (X.4). "Devotional exercises" translates Félibien's *exercices de piété*.

[273] *Constitutions*, 32–33; *Règlemens*, 66 (X.4).

[274] Gen 3:19. This is part of Adam's punishment for having eaten the forbidden fruit of the Tree of the Knowledge of Good and Evil.

[275] See Acts 18:3. What Félibien actually says is that Saint Paul made *tapisseries*, which we would normally translate as tapestries. This is obviously not the case, and the implication is that Paul was a weaver—*tapisserie* can mean weaving—who wove material (usually goats' hair) for tents.

[276] The *Constitutions*, 34, elaborate this by stating that the monks of La Trappe may not communicate with each other in any way (including written messages), still less with religious from outside or any

week, however, they gather together for the Conference, though only once [a week] in Lent.[277] This takes the place of recreation[278] and enables them to taste what pleasure there can be for a soul who loves God in listening to those to whom God has spoken speak of God. When they have all assembled in the place where the Conference is to be held,[279] the superior reads an appropriate passage, and the one to whom he then makes the sign to speak straightaway stands up and uncovers himself.[280] Then, when he has been told [by the Superior] to cover himself again and sit down, he reports what he has found

---

other person whatever, without the express permission of the abbot, and that that permission will be granted only very rarely and only when absolutely essential.

[277] This is also stated in the *Constitutions*, 35, but the *Règlemens* tell a different story. We are told there that the monks gather for the Conference each Sunday, and that if some feast day of obligation falls on a Wednesday or Thursday, on that day as well (provided the abbot thinks it fit). There are also Conferences on two other Tuesdays, those in Easter week and the week of Pentecost. But in Lent, as Félibien says, there is only one Conference a week, on Sunday. See *Règlemens*, 53 (VIII.1).

[278] The *Règlemens*, 52–53 (VIII.1), are far more forthright: "We shall use the term *Conference*, and never *Recreation*, which is a word unknown to our Fathers, as also what that word signifies. For in their view, all [forms of] recreation were forbidden to those retiring to a monastery, since they should have no other aim but to devote themselves entirely to penance and penitence (see n. 128 above), and to learning day by day how to die through continual mortification."

[279] The place where the Conference might be held is not specified, and could be inside or outside. The *Règlemens*, 53 (VIII.2), speak of "the room in which [the Conference] is to be held," and *Règlemens*, 55 (VIII.3), tell us that all the regulations set forth "are to be observed wherever the Conference is held, whether in the house [i.e., the abbey], or in some part of the garden, or elsewhere (*ailleurs*)." See further n. 292 below.

[280] I.e., pulls back his hood.

to be most moving[281] in his reading,[282] and ends by making a bow to the Superior. Those who have something to say rise to their feet to ask permission.[283]

All this takes place with much kindness, self-control, and the deference that each has for the others, and if by chance someone wishes to say something, the one who is speaking immediately ceases so as to allow the other freedom to speak. But if it happens that someone has reason to insist on what he would like to say, he may not do so more than twice, and those

---

[281] *Plus touchant*, which the *Constitutions*, 36, expands to *plus touchant et de plus portant à Dieu*, which we would have to paraphrase as "most effective in carrying him towards God." The *Règlemens*, 54 (VIII.3), have *de plus édifiant* (edifying) *et de plus portant à Dieu*. Being "touched" or "moved" was an essential feature of seventeenth-century spirituality. Any preacher worth his salt had to be able to appeal to the feelings and emotions of his congregation with words and gestures that touched or moved the heart. As Joris Van Eijnatten has said, "A sermon failing to appeal to the emotions was considered barren" (Joris Van Eijnatten, "Reaching Audiences: Sermons and Oratory in Europe, 1660–1800," in *The Cambridge History of Christianity, Volume VII: Enlightenment, Reawakening and Revolution 1660–1815*, ed. Stewart J. Brown and Timothy Tackett [Cambridge: Cambridge University Press, 2006], 138). It was, in any case, an emotional age. Tears flowed more freely than they do with us, and sentiment was often mistaken for conviction. There is no doubt that a sermon by one of the great preachers—Bossuet or Bourdaloue, for example, or, later, Massillon—could be effective, that he could truly touch the hearts of those who heard him, and there is no doubt that his audience wished to be touched and moved. They wanted preaching that stirred the soul, showed them their faults, rebuked them for their errors, brought tears to their eyes, and offered them hope. At La Trappe, the preachers were either the abbot or the books the monks read for their *lectio divina*, but the principle is exactly the same.

[282] I.e., his *lectio divina*: see n. 92 above.

[283] *Constitutions*, 34–36; *Règlemens*, 52–55 (VIII.1–3).

who would challenge this by stubbornly persisting in their opinions are severely rebuked.[284]

In this way these anchorites put themselves above the wiles of the devil. When he sees what great good comes from the exchanges in these Conferences on divine subjects, he tries to interrupt their course by the spirit of contention[285] and by sowing the seeds of dispute. But at La Trappe, the brothers have been perfectly educated in the school of Christianity, in which [is taught] the art of believing, praying, humiliating oneself, and loving God and one's neighbor.

[In the Conferences] one never speaks of oneself, nor of anyone else; neither [does one speak] of the affairs of the Order or of the house.[286] The subjects for each Conference are taken from Saint John Climacus, Cassian, the lives of the holy fathers of the Desert, Saint Basil, Saint Bernard, and other holy fathers of the Church.[287] Since all the brothers take great care to

---

[284] This is repeated in the *Constitutions*, 37, but the *Règlemens*, 57 (VIII.5), state that "if there are grounds for insisting on what has been said, this is not to be done more than once."

[285] Phil 2:3.

[286] Both the *Constitutions*, 39–40, and the *Règlemens*, 55–58 (VIII.4–7), give considerably more information on what subjects are to be avoided at the Conferences.

[287] The *Constitutions*, 38–39, repeat this list, but change "Saint Basil" to "Saint Basil in his monastic treatises," and add "the treatises of the *Bibliothèque ascétique*." The *Règlemens*, 57 (VIII.6), have the "Ascetic treatises of Saint Basil," and add Saint Ephrem. The monastic or ascetic treatises of Saint Basil are also most certainly *Les Ascétiques ou Traittez spirituels de St Basile le Grand, évesque de Césarée en Cappadoce*, translated by Godefroi Hermant (Paris: J. Du Puis, 1673). A copy was in the La Trappe library: see Bell, *Library*, 315 (B.35). As to Ephraem Syrus or Ephraem of Edessa, the *Divins opuscules et exercices spirituels du très saint Père Efrem, archediacre d'Edesse en Mésopotamie . . . par F. François Feu-Ardent de l'Ordre de S. François*, had been published at Paris by Sébastien Nivelle in 1579, and the *IV Discours de la componction, par S. Ephrem le Syrien*, translated by Jean Bosquillon, had first

preserve the harmonious unity[288] they have among them, neither at the Conference nor anywhere else do they ever say or do anything that might indicate some particular friendship or liking for one person more than another.[289]

As soon as the bell rings to bring the Conference to an end, whoever is speaking [immediately] stops the discourse he has begun, even leaving words unfinished in order to return to an admirable silence.[290]

They do not spend the days on which there are no Conferences without benefiting from a period of solitude. And if they

---

appeared in 1685 (Paris: J. Le Febvre). The 1675 edition of the Latin translation of Ephraem by Gerardus Vossius / Gerhard Voss—*Sancti Ephraem Syri . . . Opera Omnia*—was in the library of La Trappe (Bell, *Library*, 392 [E.3]), but the *Règlemens*, 57 (VIII.5), state that in the Conferences "one may not cite any passage in Latin without permission, which should be granted only rarely." The "treatises of the *Bibliothèque ascétique*" cannot refer to the *Bibliothèque ascétique* of the Augustinian Dom Jérôme, nor the *Bibliotheca Ascetica* of the Benedictine Bernhard Pez, both multivolume works, since neither was published before the eighteenth century. If it refers to a section of the La Trappe library containing ascetic works, then this is the only evidence we have for such a section. Further on what books the monks of La Trappe might or might not read, see Bell, *Library*, 63–69.

[288] "Harmonious unity" translates Félibien's *union*.

[289] "Particular friendships," which might lead to illicit sexual intimacy, were always a source of concern for any abbot—Pachomius himself warns against them—and great care was taken at La Trappe to reduce to an absolute minimum the possibility of such friendships. The *Constitutions*, 41, add here "for there is nothing more ruinous to unity and charity, and then to whatever good there is in a community, than particular friendships."

[290] *Constitutions*, 42; *Règlemens*, 59 (VIII.7). In the *Règlemens*, there is no mention of a bell: the superior makes a sign to finish the Conference. The same Regulation also states that the Conference should never last more than an hour, unless a longer time is required for some extraordinary reason.

need to take a walk, they go to a place in the woods a short distance from the house that is not frequented by seculars, and there, separated from one another, they occupy themselves with reading for the space of an hour and a half. After this the superior knocks, and each brother comes to him to discuss what he has just read, and afterwards, a quarter of an hour before Vespers,[291] they return [to the house] in the same silence as before.[292]

What a great pleasure it is to speak of God in this way! But—alas!—it is unknown to worldly people to whom God is unknown.

---

[291] Félibien has already told us that Vespers were at 4 p.m.

[292] This paragraph echoes the *Constitutions*, 43–44, but it is no more than a brief summary of the much longer section in the later *Règlemens*, 60–62 (IX), dealing with these outdoor walks. Rancé did not like them. The Regulations tell us that although most monastic congregations and observances introduced these walks "under the pretext of necessity," there were always problems. "Instead of refreshing the monks and giving them solace, as was supposed to be the case, [these walks] produced a laxity and liberty contrary to their spirit, which is not at all appropriate for persons of their profession. Nevertheless, we have not refused permission to our religious to go out all together now and then (*quelquefois*) to hold the Conference in the woods, but in such a way, and under such circumstances, that made [the Conference] useful and that prevented all evil effects." This is then followed by details as to how exactly the Conferences were to be conducted, and further cautions about how often they should be held, namely, four or five times at most in any year. "For just as we believe walks to be useful when they are rare, we are also convinced that they cannot be frequent without making the religious lose their taste for the cloister, without making them less recollected and less interior, and without casting them into [spiritual] apathy [*langueur*], and giving them desires and longings to seek outside their monastic enclosures comforts forbidden to them, [comforts] of which they are no longer permitted to think."

[Of (the Chapter of) Faults]

There is no surer way of having a person draw our attention to our faults than to inform him of his own, and this is one of the main motives one must have when [practising] that brotherly correction laid down for us in the Gospel.[293] This is why the Chapter of Faults[294] is held twice a week at La Trappe—namely, on Wednesdays and Saturdays[295]—and it is at that time that those who have noticed some fault or other on the part of their brothers can proclaim them. Even the superior is not exempt.

One can only accuse oneself of exterior faults against the Rule, the Constitutions and Customs of the house, or particular rulings of the superior,[296] and this accusation is made only with a view to pleasing Jesus Christ, who gave us mutual jurisdiction over each other and imposed upon us the duty to correct and to be corrected.[297] Before beginning the accusation, they all prostrate themselves, and the Superior says *Quid dicite?* ["What do you have to say?"] Then, in a very low voice, each one replies *Culpas meas* ["My faults"].[298] After this one sees a wholly divine zeal triumph in the heart of these anchorites, and they feel its effects in a Christian charity that allows them to say with complete freedom "I proclaim Brother N."[299]

---

[293] Matt 18:15; Luke 17:3.

[294] The Chapter of Faults is the subject of the lengthy section in the *Règlemens*, 41–49 (VII.1–8). It is based on the *Ecclesiastica officia*, 70.44–62 (Choisselet/Vernet, 204–7).

[295] This is also stated in the *Constitutions*, 44, but according to the *Règlemens*, 48 (VII.7), "the Chapter of Faults is held every day, except Sundays and Holy Days of Obligation."

[296] *Constitutions*, 46; *Règlemens*, 42 (VII.2).

[297] See n. 293 above.

[298] *Constitutions*, 45–46; *Règlemens*, 41–42 (VII.1).

[299] *Constitutions*, 47. According to the *Règlemens*, 46 (VII.4), "Before proclaiming one another, we say out loud: 'I proclaim Dom N.' or 'my Brother N.'" The title Dom (from the Latin *dominus*, "lord,

The brother who has been accused, however, remains prostrate until the superior has him rise to his feet and come before him to hear the fault for which he has been proclaimed. But what depths of humility can be seen in accuser and accused: the latter never makes excuses for himself, and the former simply states the facts as they occurred, adding nothing that would either magnify or lessen [the fault].[300]

What can we say after this about brotherly correction—save that it is a shrewd and holy technique [given us] by Jesus Christ to enable Christians to recognize and correct their slightest imperfections. He has allowed each one of us to alert his neighbor to whatever he sees as being defective in him, for we are all clear sighted when it comes to the defects of others, and from the moment that we alert others to their defects, they become more clear sighted in alerting us to ours.

It is much to be wished that we in the world would avail ourselves of this salutary technique [given us] by the Lord, and, indeed, that we should practise humility here as [it is practised] at La Trappe. But we correct no one, because we do not wish to be corrected ourselves.

[The Infirmary]

It is very difficult to decide whether one should wish for illness or fear it. We know from experience that someone who retires to bed in almost perfect health often wakes up much debilitated, and sometimes never recovers their former spark.

---

master") indicates an ordained priest. And, we are told, we may never proclaim a brother by whom we ourselves have been proclaimed on the same day.

[300] *Constitutions*, 47–49; *Règlemens*, 46–47 (VII.4–5), both of which state that the fault may not be magnified or lessened "by interpreting the intention of the brother proclaimed, either to his advantage or his disadvantage."

We know only too well that the greatest saints, after having resisted the most formidable temptations, succumb to illnesses that come upon them unexpectedly.

In order to avoid this misfortune, the monks of La Trappe abandon themselves to the invisible guidance of God by submitting themselves to the visible guidance of their superior. Nor are they permitted to take greater care of themselves when they are ill than when they are well.

This is why they do not fail to inform the Superior if they are struck by some malady without waiting for him to anticipate them. After that, they remain at peace and quite indifferent to whatever may befall them.[301]

This holy indifference to life or death, sickness or health, which is demanded of them, lets us see clearly that the spirit of La Trappe lies in the unceasing practice of virtue, lest any be taken by surprise. The example of Job teaches these anchorites that sickness is the last resort of the Devil,[302] and they need to be more vigilant than ever in overcoming the last attack of this roaring lion who is ever going about seeking whom he may devour.[303]

But at La Trappe, the terrifying efforts he makes by having them suffer such grievous illnesses are all in vain, for this holy place is the reef on which his hopes [founder] through the vigilance of Monsieur l'Abbé and the humility of the monks.

Just as they may not ask for any medication themselves, so too they cannot refuse any that is presented to them.[304] This

---

[301] *Constitutions*, 51–52; *Règlemens*, 76 (XII.1). The brothers must disclose to their superior all their bodily infirmities, however minor, with as much care as they should have in hiding them from everyone else. In other words, the abbot must know exactly what is going on in his abbey.

[302] In the book of Job, Satan (with God's permission) takes away Job's wealth and property, his children, and his bodily health.

[303] 1 Pet 5:8.

[304] Presented to them, that is, by order of the superior: see *Constitutions*, 52, and *Règlemens*, 76 (XII.2).

would show that they are giving in to the senses, and a refusal would be regarded as resulting from the fact that one did not like the taste of the medicaments.[305]

[Those in the infirmary] never show the slightest concern about what they eat, and they take great care not to fall into the bad habits of those invalids of little virtue who love [to have] a change in their meals, whether it be in the food they eat or the time at which they eat it.[306] And far from enjoying delicate foods, they content themselves with the coarsest victuals, and never ever take fruit preserves or anything sweetened with sugar.[307]

If one visits these invalids at that time of the Conference, there must be no discussion of their illness; neither may [those visiting] express any opinion regarding the state of their health. The conversation may only be about holy things.[308]

Finally, we may say that these [men] are angels on earth whose spirit is always borne up to God and who could not live a single moment if they were to be deprived of the happiness of loving him and adoring him without cease. The excessive nature of the ills that befall them, even the approach of death itself, is unable to distract them by the slightest amount from this continual exercise. And despite their poor physical condi-

---

[305] *Constitutions*, 52–53; *Règlemens*, 76 (XII.1). The objection one normally has to taking medicine is that it tastes awful. But this is to give in to *sensualité* and indicates "a hidden pride that leads us to refuse permitted and legitimate relief."

[306] *Constitutions*, 55–56; *Règlemens*, 78 (XII.3).

[307] *Constitutions*, 58; *Règlemens*, 79 (XII.4). I have translated *confitures* as fruit preserves. One might also say jams.

[308] *Constitutions*, 59. The *Règlemens*, 83–84 (XII.8), state that no one may enter the infirmary without the superior's permission, and that permission to speak to any one of the invalids should be given very rarely, and only to those whose conversation might be useful and helpful to the sick. Useful and helpful, that is, in carrying him towards God (*pour le porter à Dieu*: see n. 281 above) and inspiring him with patience in his sufferings.

tion, one very often sees them making astonishing efforts to get themselves to church at the times of the Office,[309] and, once there, penetrated by a wholly divine zeal, to praise God, offering him thanks for that with which he has visited them, and asking him for the strength to do penance[310] worthy of eternal salvation.

Usual Practices at the Abbey of La Trappe[311]

1. If anyone breaks silence, or even if he speaks loudly [when discussing] necessary matters, he fasts on bread and water.[312]

2. Since there is nothing so scandalous as to hear a monk speaking unkindly, they take care that when the brothers, and especially the novices, reply to something, they do not do so too sharply.[313]

3. If a monk should be forcefully reproved by his Superior, wherever the place and meeting may be, he must immediately prostrate himself and remain in that position until he is ordered to rise to his feet.[314]

4. They may never speak other than well of a person, and as soon as a brother has spoken a harsh word to another, he prostrates himself at his feet.[315]

---

[309] We may recall Félibien's account of the last hours of Dom Jacques Minguet.

[310] *Pénitence*: see n. 128 above.

[311] These eight regulations are an abbreviated version of the longer section in the *Constitutions*, 67–75, entitled "Some Practices." Chapter XIV in the *Règlemens*, 91–101 (XIV.1–15), "Some Regulations and General Practices" (which we discussed in the Introduction) is longer still.

[312] *Constitutions*, 67; *Règlemens*, 91 (XIV.1).

[313] *Constitutions*, 68–69; *Règlemens*, 94 (XIV.3).

[314] *Constitutions*, 71. This does not appear in the *Règlemens*.

[315] *Constitutions*, 70; *Règlemens*, 94 (XIV.3).

5. Just as one should have compassion for faults committed through weakness, one is courageously and inflexibly firm in repressing those that arise from malice or pride.[316]

6. When anyone has broken or lost something at work or elsewhere, he goes to the superior, or whoever is deputizing for him, and falls to his knees before him.[317]

7. One never calls anyone from afar, either by voice or any other sound.[318]

8. No one excuses himself from faults for which he has been reproved, whether he has actually committed them or not. The desire to make excuses for oneself is regarded as a sin.[319]

The End

---

[316] *Constitutions*, 70; *Règlemens*, 94–95 (XIV.4).

[317] *Constitutions*, 72–73. This does not appear in Chapter XIV of the *Règlemens* but echoes *Règlemens*, 19 (III.5), and 69 (X.9).

[318] *Constitutions*, 74. *Règlemens*, 92 (XIV.1), states, "One never calls anyone from afar, either by voice or by clapping one's hands, excepting the superior."

[319] *Constitutions*, 74–75, the very end of the book, which adds that any such excuse is to be considered a violation of the instruction given in the fourth degree of humility of the Rule of Saint Benedict, namely, that if one is the subject of injustice, it should be borne in silence and patience (RB 7.35). The same text appears in the *Règlemens*, 47 (VII.6), but in its proper place, namely, the section on the Chapter of Faults. Félibien's word for sin is *crime*: see n. 152 above.

APPENDIX

DISCOURSE ON THE REFORM OF THE ABBEY OF LA TRAPPE
Constitutions de l'abbaye de La Trappe
(Paris: Michel Le Petit & Estienne Michallet, 1671),
unpaginated preface.

It has always been true that, since the time that monastic orders first came into being, God has from time to time raised up holy people who have reestablished the ancient discipline. The Order of Cîteaux provides us with examples from a number of different centuries, for it produced four important reforms: the Congregation of Castile,[1] [the Congregation] of Lombardy,[2]

---

[1] Of the three Congregations founded in the Iberian Peninsula, the Congregation of Castile was the only one that came into being from a real desire for reform. The other two—the Congregation of Aragon and Navarre and the Congregation of Alcobaça—were more concerned with questions of political and ecclesiastical independence. The Congregation of Castile was founded in 1427 by Martin de Vargas, originally a Hieronymite who became a Cistercian monk in the monastery of Piedra, and his reform proved remarkably successful. The Congregation was suppressed in 1835. See further Lekai, *Cistercians*, 128–30.

[2] The Congregation of Lombardy, more accurately the Congregation of Saint Bernard in Italy, came into being in 1497 when it was approved by Pope Alexander VII. The moving force behind its foundation was the duke of Milan, Ludovico Sforza, and the new Congregation united eight monasteries from the Province of Lombardy and seven from the Province of Tuscany. The new Congregation restored regular monastic observance, which had been

[the reform] of the Feuillants,³ and the [reform of the] Strict Observance of the Bernardines of France, with which is associated the abbey of Our Lady of La Trappe, whose Constitutions are here set forth.

This abbey lies on the border of the Perche and Normandy in the diocese of Sens, three leagues⁴ from Mortagne[-au-Perche]. Rotrou, count of the Perche, founded it in 1140,⁵ and, in accordance with the ancient Usage of Cîteaux,⁶ it is situated in an unpopulated valley. For many centuries, the dominant features [of life at the abbey] were license and laxity, but in our days it has embraced once again the first zeal of its founders, for the abbot who governs [the house] now⁷ makes the pure Rule of Saint Benedict flourish once again, in such a way that one sees God everywhere at the abbey, just as was said of Clairvaux long ago. Thus, whoever wishes to take up residence

---

seriously affected by the ravages of the commendatory system in Italy, and provided a system of mutual assistance between its affiliated houses. See further Lekai, *Cistercians*, 130–31.

³ The Feuillants were founded by Jean de La Barrière (1544–1600), commendatory abbot of Feuillant, a Cistercian abbey near Toulouse that, at the time, was in much the same state of decay as La Trappe before Rancé. Like Rancé, La Barrière underwent a conversion, joined the Cistercians in 1573, and set about reforming his abbey. Those who did not wish for reform were removed, and from 1577 La Barrière instituted a program of fierce austerity and demanding asceticism. His reform, like that of the Congregation of Castile, was remarkably successful, and the Feuillants remained a flourishing Congregation until they were suppressed, with all the other monastic orders in France, at the Revolution. See further Lekai, *Cistercians*, 135–37.

⁴ The length of the league (*lieue*) varied from time to time and from place to place in France, but Mortagne is just about fifteen kilometers from La Trappe.

⁵ See n. 29 to the Introduction.

⁶ See *Exordium Cistercii*, I; Waddell, *Texts*, 178–79, 400–401, with the accompanying note. The *Exordium*, *Summa Cartae caritatis*, and *Capitula* are referred to as the *Usus Cisterciensium monachorum* (Waddell, *Texts*, 179, 399).

⁷ I.e., Rancé.

in the monastery of La Trappe should bring with him only his soul: the flesh has no part to play in there. They are engaged in praying, in fasting, and in manual labor, following the maxim of the ancient solitaries of Egypt, [namely,] that a monk whose time is fully occupied is tempted by only a single demon. [The monastery] is not the place to look after your health, nor to examine the various qualities of the food. If you should say that cheese overloads the stomach, think, I beg you, on the immediate response you will get: You are a monk, not a physician. It is not your business to judge your state of health, but rather your [monastic] profession and the state [of your soul]. Religious houses should be schools of penitence, for the entire knowledge of the saints consists in this: to suffer mortifications for a time, in order to enjoy delights for eternity.

Yet to the great scandal of the Church, idleness, self-indulgence, vanity, and worldly intrigue now reign in most cloisters. Silence, humility, withdrawal [from the world], and manual labor have been virtually banished. And if someone there occupies himself with literature, it is most often for the sake of ambition or empty curiosity. Thus it follows that many of our monks, enchanted by the love of the world, are unfaithful to God, and all they reserve for him is their [monastic] habit and their tonsure! For them, the monastery is a hell. They themselves are dry and sterile when it comes to the gifts of grace, for this oil from heaven fills only empty vessels and not those who, on the contrary, are filled with the love of created things and leave no point of entry for heavenly and divine consolations. A monk will convert more souls by praying to God for them in his cell than by coming out of his solitude to preach. "What are you doing in the towns?" says Saint Jerome to these wandering monks. "The bishops and priests have the apostles as their models, but you have as your masters the Hilarions and Antonies."[8] "You are almost as far from God as

---

[8] Jerome, *Ep.* 58.5 *ad Paulinum*; PL 22:583.

you are far from your monastery," said Saint Bernard. "And it follows from this," he adds, "that when we leave our solitude we become chatterboxes, given over to curiosity,[9] mockery, and slander, we amuse ourselves with mere vanities and flee the labors of [monastic] discipline."[10] Alas! If you only knew what is the real duty of a monk, you would water with your tears all the bread that you eat,[11] for one enters the religions life only to weep for one's own sins and those of others.

A well-regulated[12] monastery is a perfect image of Paradise. One lives there in holy concord, one is careful to do nothing that is displeasing to God, and since the superiors there are edifying and embraced by charity, they find [their monks] ready and willing to obey them. The abbey of La Trappe enjoys the same happy success, and we may certainly believe that it will possess this felicity for many centuries[13] since it conforms entirely to the first spirit of the Order of Cîteaux[14] and avoids any intercourse with the world, which usually opens the door to disorder and a failure to keep the Rule.[15]

We know well that there are many who disparage the austerities practised there, for the well-regulated life[16] they see there is a tacit condemnation of their own self-indulgence and laxity. But you, my God, who enter into the very depths of the

---

[9] Curiosity (*curiositas* in Latin) is always bad: see n. 71 to the translation.

[10] The writer is paraphrasing Bernard, *In Annuntiatione dominica*, S 3.9; SBOp 5:41.

[11] See Pss 41:3; 79:6; 101:10.

[12] *Bien reglé*: i.e., a monastery that keeps its rule, in this case, the Rule of Saint Benedict.

[13] It possessed it for more than a century before being suppressed at the French Revolution in 1790.

[14] See n. 23 to the translation.

[15] "disorder and a failure to keep the rule" is a long-winded translation of *dérèglement*, but that is the meaning of the word here.

[16] "well-regulated life" translates *régularité*: see nn. 12 and 15 above.

Appendix: Discourse on the Reform of the Abbey of La Trappe 159

heart,[17] you know those who seek only your interests and those who seek their own. It is said that the fervor [one sees at the abbey] is too passionate to be able to last long. Yet far from being strangled at its birth, it continues to exist and has already transmitted its zeal to other monasteries, for the abbey of Sept-Fons in Bourbonnais[18] and that of Bonnaigue in the Limousin[19] imitate its example and follow just the same way of life.

Moreover, we will not speak here of those many religious of other orders who have set out to embrace the reform. It is not there that one cultivates the most skilled culinary arts so that the fish and eggs are tastily prepared, and the exquisite dishes fatten the body and not the soul. A few vegetables, bread, and cider will disgust those who do nothing, but to those who work they are a feast. You fear the weight of the austerities, yet they are light to those who think about [avoiding] hell! When you remember that you will have to render account for all your careless words,[20] you will never worry

---

[17] See 1 Cor 2:9.
[18] Sept-Fons in the diocese of Autun was reformed by Dom Eustache de Beaufort, who was appointed commendatory abbot in 1656 at the age of twenty, embraced the reform of Rancé early in 1664, and began the transformation of what, at the time, was "a poor, scarcely habitable and depopulated monastery" (Lekai, *Rise*, 204). By Beaufort's death in 1709 there were some 120 professed religious at Sept-Fons, and the house continued to flourish throughout the eighteenth century. It still does, after having been refounded in the nineteenth century. See further Lekai, *Rise*, 204, and page 104 of his index.
[19] Bonnaigue in the diocese of Limoges had been *in commendam* since 1492 and by the mid-seventeenth century was in deplorable condition. It was reformed by Marc-Philippe de Montroux-Peyrissac, at first commendatory abbot and then regular abbot, but the reform did not really bear fruit until it was assisted by Dom Eustache de Beaufort of Sept-Fons (see n. 18 above). But as Louis Lekai has said, "the community never emerged from mediocrity" (Lekai, *Rise*, 191).
[20] See Matt 12:36.

about silence! Tell me rather: which is best fitted to save us, a life given over to sensual pleasures and delights, or a life devoted to penance and mortification? Think well on this as you read these godly Constitutions, for this is the reason that they are being put before you: so that by detaching yourselves from the deceptions of the world, you might attach yourselves to the things of heaven.

Select Bibliography

Bell, David N. *The Library of the Abbey of La Trappe from the Twelfth Century to the French Revolution, with an Annotated Edition of the 1752 Catalogue.* Turnhout: Brepols/Cîteaux – Commentarii cistercienses, 2014.

———. *Understanding Rancé. The Spirituality of the Abbot of La Trappe in Context.* Cistercian Studies Series 205. Kalamazoo, MI: Cistercian Publications, 2005.

Charencey, Charles-Félix-Hyacinthe, comte de. *Histoire de l'abbaye de la Grande-Trappe.* Documents sur la Province du Perche; ii, 6. Mortagne: Georges Meaux, 1896–1911.

Choisselet, Danièle, and Placide Vernet, eds. *Les Ecclesiastica Officia cisterciens du XIIème siècle.* La Documentation cistercienne, 22. Reiningue: Abbaye d'Œlenberg, 1989.

Constitutions de l'abbaye de La Trappe. Paris: Michel Le Petit & Estienne Michallet, 1671.

Dubois, Louis. *Histoire civile, religieuse et littéraire de l'abbaye de La Trappe, et des autres Monastères de la même Observance qui se sont établis tant en France que dans les pays étrangers avant et depuis la révolution de 1789, et notamment de l'Abbaye de Mellerai; suivie de chartes et d'autres pièces justificatives, la plupart inédites.* Paris: Raynal, 1824.

———. *Histoire de l'abbé de Rancé et de sa réforme.* 2nd ed. Paris: Poussielgue Frères, 1869.

Dubois, Marie-Gérard, Alban J. Krailsheimer, Augustin-Hervé Laffay, Hugues de Seréville, and Philippe Siguret. *L'Abbaye Notre-Dame de La Trappe.* Meaucé: Amis du Perche, 2001.

Gervaise, Armand-François. *Jugement critique, mais équitable des vies de feu M. l'abbé de Rancé, réformateur de l'abbaye de La Trappe. Écrites par les Sieurs Marsollier et Maupeou. Divisé en deux parties où l'on voit toutes les fautes qu'ils ont commises contre la vérité de l'Histoire, contre le bon sens, contre la vraysemblence [sic], contre l'honneur même de M. de Rancé, et de la Maison de La Trappe.* London [= Troyes or Reims]: [n.p.], 1742.

Krailsheimer, Alban J. *Armand-Jean de Rancé, Abbot of La Trappe. His Influence in the Cloister and the World.* Oxford: Clarendon Press, 1974.

———. *Rancé and the Trappist Legacy.* CS 86. Kalamazoo, MI: Cistercian Publications, 1985.

Lekai, Louis J. *The Cistercians. Ideals and Reality.* Kent, OH: Kent State University Press, 1977.

———. *The Rise of the Cistercian Strict Observance in Seventeenth Century France.* Washington, DC: Catholic University of America Press, 1968.

Rancé, Armand-Jean de. *Abbé de Rancé. Correspondance.* Ed. Alban J. Krailsheimer. Paris: Les Éditions du Cerf / Cîteaux – Commentarii cistercienses, 1993.

———. *Règlemens de l'abbaye de Nôtre-Dame de La Trappe en forme de Constitutions, avec des Réflexions, Et la Carte de Visite faite à N. D. des Clairets, par le R. P. Abbé de la Trappe.* Paris: Florentin Delaulne, 1718.

Tournoüer, Henri. *Bibliographie et iconographie de la Maison-Dieu Notre-Dame de La Trappe au diocèse de Sées, de Dom A.-J. Le Bouthillier de Rancé, Abbé et Réformateur de cette abbaye, et en général de tous les religieux du même monastère. Documents sur la province du Perche*; iv, 2. Mortagne: Marchand & Gilles/Georges Meaux, 1894–1896.

Waddell, Chrysogonus. *Narrative and Legislative Texts from Early Cîteaux. Latin Text in Dual Edition with English Translation and Notes.* Studia et Documenta, IX. Brecht: Cîteaux – Commentarii cistercienses, 1999.

Index of Subjects

Agreement (*concordat*) between Rancé and former monks of La Trappe, 53 n. 26
Almoner, duties of, 50–51 n. 20
Amour, 85 n. 105
Apples, 82, 84, 87
Artichokes, 82
Asparagus, 82

Baptism, 129
Beds and bedclothes, 85, 133
Beer, 81 n. 94, 135
Beetroots, 82
Books: reading, writing, binding, 77–78
  See also Reading
Bread, 65, 69, 81–82, 84, 87, 134, 159
Butter, 69 n. 67, 82, 135, 137

Carrots, 82, 135 n. 233
Cellarer, 32, 76 n. 86, 137 n. 264, 139
Chant and chanting, 79, 80, 87, 130
Chapter of Faults, 116–17 nn. 168–69, 148–49, 153 n. 319
Charité, 85 n. 105
Cheese, 135, 136, 157
Church at La Trappe, description of, 71–76

Cider, 65, 69, 81, 84, 159
Clocks, 59 n. 42
Cloisters, 139–39
Collation, 81 n. 95, 84–85, 135
Commendatory abbots and the commendatory system, 17, 36, 51 n. 21, 156 n. 2
Compline, Office of, 81, 85
Conferences, 39, 94, 138, 142–47
Confession, 77, 83, 102, 108, 122–23
Conversi. See Laybrothers
Cook, 136–37
Cowl, 77, 84, 131 n. 203, 139, 140 n. 264
Curiosity, condemned, 71 n. 71, 133, 158

Daily schedule, 76–80, 130–31
Description of La Trappe in the 1660s, 20–21, 23
Diet, 81–82, 134–36
Dormitory, 39, 76–77 n. 84, 85, 110 n. 158, 130 n. 200, 132–33
Doves and dovecotes, 48 n. 11
Dowry, monastic, 126

Eating in the refectory, 134–36
Eggs, 48 n. 11, 58, 59 n. 42, 69, 85, 135, 159

Fasts and fasting, 80, 81 n. 95, 82, 84, 86, 110, 112, 115, 118, 134–35, 152, 157
Fish, 58, 59 n. 42, 64, 69–70, 135, 159
Flagellation, 119
Food and drink served to guests, 69–70
Fruits, 63, 75 (sugared), 134–36, 151 (fruit preserves)

Garden, the abbey, 47, 49, 66, 82, 139, 140, 141, 143 n. 279
Gruel, 82, 135
Guests, behavior of, 66
Guests, welcoming of, 65–66, 68–69

Handkerchiefs, 110 n. 158
Hemina, its quantity, 58 n. 41
High altar, description of, 73–75
History of La Trappe, 12–17
Humiliations, 23–24, 87–88, 109, 116
Humility, 43, 44, 69, 79, 88, 90, 108, 110, 114–15, 120, 123, 127, 149, 150, 153 n. 319, 157
See also Humiliations

Infirmarian, 132 n. 210
Infirmary, 85, 120 n. 179, 121, 123, 124, 149–52
Isolation of La Trappe, 46 n. 4, 47

Joy of the monks, 79–80, 87, 95, 105, 117, 124

King (Louis XIV), prayers for the, 95
Kitchen servers, 136–37, 139

Latin, 100 n. 135, 129 n. 196, 146 n. 287, 148 n. 299, 158 n. 9
Lauds, Office of, 136 n. 239
Lawsuits and legal proceedings, 91–94
Laxity in observing the Rule, 22, 50, 88, 147 n. 292, 156, 158
Laybrothers (*conversi*), 21, 48, 52 n. 22, 64 n. 53, 65 n. 54, 72, 82, 136, 142
Library at La Trappe, 39 n. 95, 54 n. 32, 55, 58 n. 41, 100 n. 134, 125, 145–46 n. 287
Linen, 85
Little Office of the Blessed Virgin Mary, 76 m. 83, 116 n. 167

Mandatum (foot washing), 136 n. 239
Manual labor, 59–60 n. 43, 66, 77–78, 83–84, 87, 88, 99, 139–42, 157
Manuscripts, 78 n. 87
Matins, Office of, 76, 79, 116, 130
Mattresses, 85, 133
Meat, 48 n. 11, 58 n. 42, 85, 120 n. 179
Milk and milk products, 82, 135
Mortality at La Trappe, 28–29, 98 n. 131
Mortifications, 97–98, 99–104, 107–13, 115–24, 127–28, 141, 160

Novices, 22, 29, 34–35, 37, 38, 56, 64 n. 53, 83, 85, 87–88, 103, 115, 116, 126, 136, 139, 152

Index of Subjects

Numbers of monks and laybrothers, 28, 64 n. 53
Nuts, 84

Oatmeal, 82, 135

Parlor, 89–90, 139
Particular friendships, 146 n. 289
Pears, 82, 84, 87
Penitence/penance, 11, 43, 58, 79 n. 90, 88, 89, 97, 102, 103–8, 109, 111, 112, 113, 115, 119, 120, 124, 129, 130, 133, 142, 143, 152, 157, 160
Perseverance, 105 n. 149
Pillows, 48 n. 11, 85
Porter, 48 n. 10, 65, 66, 68, 69 n. 66, 82, 99
Potatoes, 135 n. 233
Poultry, 58 n. 42, 85
Prayer and praying, 69 n. 66, 76, 78 n. 88, 82, 95, 101, 108, 109, 111, 112, 115, 116, 117, 119, 121, 124, 131, 145, 157
Prime, Office of, 59 n. 43, 76, 77, 116
Providence, its nature and importance, 63 n. 50, 66, 92, 119
Public fascination with La Trappe, 43–44
Purgatory, 121

Rancé's unfinished dwelling at La Trappe, 71
Reading, 80 n. 92, 83, 84, 85, 100, 147
Reading in the refectory, 70, 82
Recollection, 86 n. 106, 131, 139, 147 n. 292

Recreation, 143
Refectorian, 137
Refectory, description of, 81, 88, 133–37
Rice, 135

Sacristan, 76 n. 86, 131 n. 202, 137
Scapular, 140
Seal of La Trappe, 125
Self-will, 98 n. 130
Sermons, 77
Sext, Office of, 28, 78, 80
Shoes, 138
Sign language, 140, 143
Silence, 66, 68, 87, 131, 138, 140, 142, 147, 152, 157, 160
Simplicity, 75–76, 92, 116, 132
Slippers, 138
Spittoons, 110 n. 158, 131 n. 202
Sugar, 85, 151

Tabernacle, location of, 73–74
Tomb, the monastery as a, 94, 127 n. 193
Transubstantiation, 74 n. 80
Trental, 122 n. 181

Vegetables, 69, 77, 78, 82, 84, 88, 120, 135, 137, 159
Vespers, Office of, 59 n. 43, 81, 84, 101, 102, 147
Viaticum, 112, 123

Warming room, 77, 138
Watermill, 48 n. 13, 84 n. 101
Welcoming guests, 65–66, 68–69
Wine, 58, 70, 81 n. 94, 83, 84 n. 101, 97, 112 n. 159, 134

Index of Names and Places

Abraham, patriarch, 104
Albéric, Dom, monk of
 Perseigne, 57 n. 40
Alcobaça, Congregation of, 155
 n. 1
Alexander III, pope, 15
Alexander VII, pope, 61 n. 44,
 62 n. 47, 155 n. 2
Anacreon, Greek poet, 18
Ancelin, Bernard, abbot of
 Saint-Martin, 57 n. 40
Anne of Austria, queen of
 France, 54 n. 30, 63 n. 51
Antony the Great, Saint, 157
Aragon and Navarre, Congregation of, 155 n. 1
Argentan, Louis-François d',
 Capuchin theologian, 100
 n. 134
Arnolfini, Octave, abbot of
 La Charmoye, 50 n. 17
Athenagoras of Athens, 98 n.
 130
Aubin, Laurent, publisher, 2
Augustine of Hippo, Saint, 68 n.
 65, 85 n. 105, 87 n. 107, 89,
 98 n. 130, 101, 105 n. 149

Baldwin, count of Flanders, 13
Barbeaux, Cistercian abbey, 32

Barfleur (Normandy), 13–14, 72
 n. 72
Basil the Great/Basil of
 Caesarea, Saint, 145
Bastille, the, Paris, 30
Beaufort, Eustache de,
 commendatory abbot of
 Sept-Fons, 159 n. 18, 159 n.
 19
Beauvais (Hauts-de-France), 3,
 10, 51 n. 21
Bellarmine, Robert, Saint and
 cardinal, 69 n. 66
Bellay, Jean du, commendatory
 abbot of La Trappe, 17
Bellefonds, Bernardin Gigault
 de, Marshal of France, 36
Bellefonds, Marie Gigault de,
 marquise de Villars, 36
Benedict, Rule of Saint, 32, 37,
 50, 52, 52 n. 23, 58, 58 n. 41,
 59 n. 43, 60, 64, 76 n. 84, 79,
 84 n. 102, 102, 110, 116, 116
 n. 168, 148, 153 n. 319, 156,
 158
Bernard of Clairvaux, Saint, 59
 n. 43, 68 n. 65, 75, 80 n. 92,
 97 n. 127, 125, 145, 157–58
Bernier, Joseph, monk of La
 Trappe, 53 n. 26, 102–04

Index of Names and Places

Bernières, Jean de, sieur de Louvigny, 100 n. 134
Boileau, Jean-Jacques, abbé, 12
Boniface VIII, pope, 114–15 n. 164
Bonnaigue, Cistercian abbey, 159
Bonsmoulins, château, 16
Borromeo, Charles, Saint, 74 n. 80
Bosquillon, Jean, 145–46 n. 287
Bossuet, Jacques-Bénigne, bishop of Meaux, 144 n. 281
Bouchu, Pierre IV, abbot of Clairvaux, 36, 139 n. 256
Bourdaloue, Louis, Jesuit and preacher, 144 n. 281
Boulogne, Grandmontine priory, 51 n. 21
Bourges (Centre-Val de Loire), 7
Bouthillier, Denis, Rancé's father, 17–18, 19
Bouthillier, Denis-François, Rancé's brother, 17–18, 51 n. 21
Bouthillier, Victor, archbishop of Tours, 19, 51 n. 20
Brémule, battle of (1119), 13
Breuil-Benoît, Savigniac abbey, 14, 49
Browne, Edward, English traveler, 55 n. 33

Cabala, the, 31
Caen (Normandy), 2, 52 n. 24
Cassian, John. *See* John Cassian
Castelnaudary, battle of (1632), 9
Castile, Congregation of, 155, 156 n. 3

Cawley, Martinus, 38
Celestine V, pope, 114
Celestines, 114
Charles V, king of France, 16
Chartres (Centre-Val de Loire), 52
Châtillon-en-Lorraine, Cistercian abbey, 115 n.165
Chemiré-le-Gaudin (Pays de la Loire), 105 n. 150
Cierrey, Raoul I de, bishop of Évreux, 50 n. 16
Cîteaux, Cistercian abbey, 50, 52, 54, 60, 62, 73, 81 n. 96, 139 n. 256, 155, 156, 158
Clairvaux, Cistercian abbey, 60–61 n. 44, 139 n. 256, 156
Colbert, Jean-Baptiste, Minister of Finance, 4, 6
Collège de Harcourt, Paris, 18
Collège des Bernardins, Paris. *See* Collège Saint-Bernard, Paris
Collège Saint-Bernard, Paris, 61, 61 nn. 44–45, 63 n. 51
Cossé, François de, duke of Brissac, 10
Coulton, George, 126
Courville, Xavier de, 9–10 n. 22
Couturier, Robert/Robin, prior of Perseigne, 31–32
Curthose, Robert, duke of Normandy, 12–13

Damian, Peter, Saint. *See* Peter Damian, Saint
David, king and prophet, 67
Desert Fathers, 59 n. 42, 69 n. 66, 78 n. 88, 81 n. 95, 91 n. 115, 145

Desmares, Toussaint-Guy-
  Joseph, 2–4, 11
Drummond, James, duke of
  Perth, 7–9
Dubois, Louis, biographer of
  Rancé, 7–9, 23, 35, 37, and
  passim
Du Plessis-Liancourt, Charles,
  10
Du Plessis-Liancourt,
  Henri-Roger, count of
  La Roche-Guyon, 11
Du Plessis-Liancourt, Jeanne-
  Charlotte, mademoiselle de
  La Roche-Guyon, 11–12
Du Plessis, Roger, duke of
  Liancourt and La Roche-
  Guyon, 3–4, 10–11

Edinburgh, Scotland, 8
Egypt, 157
Ephraem Syrus/Ephraem of
  Edessa, 145 n. 287
Espinay, Claude, marquis d', 9
Espinay, Françoise d', mother of
  Jeanne de Schomberg, 9
Eugenius III, pope, 15
Eusebius of Caesarea, Church
  historian, 100 n. 135

Favier, Jean, Rancé's tutor, 18 n.
  43, 34, 96 n. 126
Félibien, André, sieur des
  Avaux et de Javercy, 2, 4–7,
  12, 22, 23, 25, 28, 33, 39–40,
  and passim
Félibien, Jean-François, 7
Félibien, Michel, 7
Félibien, Pierre, friend of Rancé,
  56 n. 36

Fellowes, William D., English
  traveler, 46 n. 4, 47 nn. 5, 8
Feuillants, Order of, 156
Florence, Italy, 37
Foisil, Zozime, abbot of La
  Trappe, 23
Fontenay-Mareuil, François
  Duval, marquis de, 5
Fouquet, Nicolas, Minister of
  Finance, 6
France, 1, 3, 6, 8, 9, 10, 11, 17, 19,
  37, 40, 50, 60 n. 44, 99 n.
  133, 128, 156 n. 4
France, Gaston Jean-Baptiste de,
  duke of Orléans, 50–51 no.
  20
Francis I, king of France, 16–17
Froidmont, Cistercian abbey,
  60–61 n. 44
Fulk, count of Anjou, 13

Galen, Greek physician, 137 n.
  243
Gaultier/Gautier/Gauthier,
  Jean, prior of La Trappe, 62
  n. 48, 64 n. 52
Gauthier, Adam, abbot of
  La Trappe, 15, 49 n. 16
Giberti, Matteo, bishop of
  Verona, 74 n. 80
Georges, Dominique, abbot of
  Val-Richer, 21 n. 53, 61–62,
  62 n. 46
Gervaise, Armand-François,
  abbot of La Trappe, 23
Gregory I/Gregory the Great,
  pope, 114, 122 n. 181
Gregory XV, pope, 50 n. 17
Guiton, Michel, prior of
  Perseigne, 55–56 n. 34

Harlay de Césy, Roger de, commendatory abbot of Perseigne, 54 n. 31, 55–56 n. 34
Harlay de Champvallon, François de, archbishop of Paris, 96 n. 126
Henry I, king of England, 11–12, 72 n. 72
Henry III, king of France, 10
Henry IV, king of France, 51 n. 20
Henry, Pierre III, abbot of Clairvaux, 139 n. 256
Hilarion, Saint, 157
Hippocrates, Greek physician, 137 n. 243
Hohart/Hoart, Henri, abbot of La Trappe, 16
Honorius III, pope, 15
Hôtel-Dieu, Paris, 55 n. 33
Hugh of Saint-Victor, ps.-, 68 n. 65
Hundred Years' War, 15–16

Innocent III, pope, 15
Innocent X, pope, 2
Ireland, 57 n. 39
Isaac, son of Abraham, 104 n. 146

James II, king of England, 8
James/Jacob of Voragine, 114 n. 163
Jansenism, 2–3, 10, 11, 31, 58 n. 41
Jeremiah, prophet, 66–67
Jerome, Saint, 157
Jesuits, 2, 3
Jesus Christ, 69 n. 66, 74, 75, 103, 105, 106, 109, 115, 117, 119, 124, 142, 148, 149

Job, biblical figure, 150
John Cassian, Saint, 81 n. 95, 137 n. 243, 145
John Climacus/John of the Ladder, Saint, 145
John the Dwarf, Desert Father, 78 n. 88
Joly, Charlotte, Rancé's mother, 17–18
Jouaud, Jean VI, abbot of Prières, 53 n. 25, 56, 60–61 n. 44, 63 n. 51
Judah the Prince/Judah ha-Nasi, Rabbi, 39

Kempis, Thomas à. *See* Thomas à Kempis
Kerviche, Guillaume, sub-prior of La Trappe, 62 n. 48
Krailsheimer, Alban J., 4, 8, 17 n. 41, 18 n. 46, 25 n. 64, 31 n. 77, 32, 38, 45 n. 2, 52 n. 22, 57 n. 37, 64 n. 53, 65 n. 54, 98 n. 131

La Barrière, Jean de, commendatory abbot of Feuillant, 156
La Cour, Jacques de, abbot of La Trappe, 23
Lancelot, Claude, Jansenist, 58 n. 41
Lannoy, Anne-Élisabeth de, wife of Henri-Roger Du Plessis-Liancourt, 11
La Reynie, Gabriel-Nicolas de, lieutenant-general of police, 30
La Rochelle (Nouvelle-Aquitaine), 9

La Rochefoucauld, François de, cardinal, 50 n. 17
Larroque, Daniel de, 19–20
Lateran Council V (1514), 17
La Trappe, Notre-Dame de, Cistercian abbey, passim
Lavolle, Robert III, abbot of La Trappe, 16
Le Baube/Poulain, Robert III, archbishop of Rouen, 15, 49 n. 16
Le Febvre, Jacques, publisher, 1, 26
Le Guédois, Nicolas III, abbot of Barbery, 52 n. 24
Lekai, Louis, 61 nn. 44–45, 159 n. 19
Le Maître, Claude, abbot of Châtillon, 24
Le Masson, Innocent, general of the Carthusians, 22
Le Nain, Pierre, Rancé's biographer, 96 n. 126
Léonard, Frédéric, publisher, 1, 25
Le Roy, Guillaume, commendatory abbot of Hautefontaine, 22, 23–25, 87 n. 109
Lexington, Stephen, abbot of Clairvaux, 61 n. 45
Liancourt, château, 3–4, 10–11
Liancourt, duchess of. *See* Schomberg, Jeanne de, duchess of Liancourt
Liancourt, duke of. *See* Du Plessis, Roger, duke of Liancourt and La Roche-Guyon
Lombardy, Congregation of, 155
Louis VI, king of France, 13

Louis IX, king of France, 15
Louis XIII, king of France, 9, 51 n. 20
Louis XIV, king of France, 2, 3, 6, 36, 56 n. 34, 61 n. 44, 63 n. 51, 95 n. 125
Lucas, bishop of Évreux, 15, 49–50 n. 16
Lucifer, 114 n. 162, 150
Lyon (Auvergne-Rhône-Alpes), 2, 31

Mabillon, Jean, Maurist, 22, 126 n. 191
Marchis, Louis, monk of La Trappe, 56 n. 35
Mardick, siege of (1646), 11
Marsollier, Jaques, Rancé's biographer, 95 n. 125
Mary, the Virgin, 73–75, 76, 95 n. 125, 109, 118–19
Massillon, Jean-Baptiste, bishop of Clermont, 144 n. 281
Masson, Claude, 64 n. 53
Matilda, countess of the Perche, 13–14
McManners, John, 122–23 n. 183
Medici, Marie de, queen of France, 51 n. 20
Metz (Grand Est), 10
Milan, Italy, 74 n. 80
Minguet, Jacques, monk of La Trappe, 24 n. 61, 29, 115–24, 152 n. 309
Mishnah, the, 39
Monceaux, Guillaume, monk of La Trappe, 105–6 n. 150
Montbazon, Marie d'Avaugour de Bretagne, Madame de, 18–21

Index of Names and Places 171

Montfaucon de Villars, Nicolas-Pierre-Henri, 30–31, 34, 35, 37, 40
Montmorency, Henri II de, 9
Montroux-Peyrissac, Marc-Philippe, abbot of Bonnaigue, 159 n. 19
Mortagne (Normandy), 14, 47, 102, 156

Newman, John Henry, cardinal, 105 n. 149
Noël, Antoine, Rancé's former valet, 56 n. 35
Noës, Julien des, abbot elect of La Trappe, 16
Notre-Dame-du-Val, Augustinian abbey, 51 n. 21

Pachomius, Saint, 146 n. 289
Paris, 1, 5, 6, 7, 8, 9, 17, 18, 19, 21, 25, 26, 30, 31, 35, 47, 53, 60, 61, 63 n. 51, 81 nn. 93–94, 84 n. 101, 96 n. 126, 125
Paris, Julien, abbot of Foucarmont, 52 n. 23
Pascal, Blaise, 31
Paul, Saint, 86 n. 105, 93, 94, 106, 142
Perche, the, 13, 14, 15, 46 n. 4, 47, 49, 125 n. 190, 156
Perseigne, Cistercian abbey, 21, 22, 32, 52 nn. 22–23, 54, 55, 56 n. 35, 57 n. 40, 62 n. 48, 98–99, 102
Peter Damian, Saint, 119 n. 175
Pez, Bernhard, Benedictine historian, 146 n. 287

Pius V, pope, 74 n. 80, 76 n. 83
Plotinus, Greek philosopher, 30, 31
Plunkett, Oliver, Saint, 57 n. 39
Plunkett, Patrick, bishop of Ardagh, 57 n. 39
Pons, Antoinette de, marquise de Guercheville, 10
Port-Royal des Champs, abbey, 3, 10, 11, 12, 31, 58 n. 41
Poussin, Nicolas, painter, 6
Preully, Cistercian abbey, 32
Prudhomme, Robert, monk of La Trappe, 56 n. 35

Rambouillet, Catherine de Vivonne, marquise de, 5
Rancé, Armand-Jean de, abbot of La Trappe, 11
 as a preacher, 96
 date of his abbatial benediction, 57 n. 37
 friendship with André Félibien, 4–5
 his library, 54–55
 his signature, 125–26
 illness and death, 1, 23, 118
 life, 17–23
 reads his will, 54–55
Ravey, Robert IV, abbot of La Trappe, 16
Richelieu, Armand-Jean du Plessis, cardinal, 17, 18, 60 n. 44
Robertson, Duncan, 80 n. 92
Rome, Italy, 2, 5–6, 22, 28, 37, 55, 56 n. 36, 61 n. 44, 62, 63–64, 74 n. 80, 114
Rosicrucianism, 31

Rotrou III, count of Mortagne and lord of Nogent, 13–15, 49, 72 n. 72, 156
Rotrou IV, count of Mortagne, 15

Saint-Clémentin, Benedictine priory, 51 n. 21, 56 n. 36
Saint-Germain-des-Prés, Benedictine (Maurist) abbey, 7
Saint-Germain-en-Laye, château, 8
Saint-Martin, Benedictine (Maurist) abbey, 57
Saint Peter's Church, Drogheda, 57 n. 39
Saint-Symphorien, Benedictine abbey, 51 n. 21
Schimmelpenninck, Mary, English traveler, 11
Schomberg, Charles de, Marshal of France, 9
Schomberg, Henri de, duke of Alluyn, 9
Schomberg, Jeanne de, duchess of Liancourt, 3–4, 9–12, 44, 45
Schomberg, Jeanne-Armande de, 10
Scotland, 8
Sées (Normandy), 57 nn. 38–39
Sept-Fons, Cistercian abbey, 2, 159
Sforza, Ludovico, duke of Milan, 155 n. 2
Sylvester, bishop of Sées, 15, 49–50 n. 16

Talmud, the, 30, 31

Tamié, Cistercian abbey, 56 n. 35
Teresa of Avila, Saint, 7
Terre de Nuisement (Saint-Colombe-sur-Risle, near L'Aigle, Normandy), 53 n. 27
Tétu, Jacques, friend of Rancé, 34–35
Thomas I, count of the Perche, 15
Thomas à Kempis, 69–70
Tinchebray, battle of (1106), 13
Toulouse (Occitanie), 30
Trent, Council of (1545–1563), 4, 17

Vallet, Marie-Raphaël, 80 n. 92
Vandenbroucke, François, 87 n. 109
Van Eijnatten, Joris, 144 n. 281
Vargas, Martin de, monk of Piedra and reformer, 155 n. 1
Vaussin, Claude, abbot of Cîteaux, 60–61 n. 44, 62 n. 47, 63 n. 51
Velleius Paterculus, Gaius, Roman historian, 68 n. 65
Véretz, château, 18, 19, 20, 21, 23, 52 n. 22
Villars, Claude-Louis-Hector de, Grand Marshal of France, 36
Villars, Henri-Félix de, commendatory abbot of Montier-en-Argonne, 36–37, 40
Villars, Nicolas-Pierre-Henri Montfaucon de. *See*

Montfaucon de Villars,
   Nicolas-Pierre-Henri
Villars, Pierre, marquis de, 36
Villiers, George, duke of
   Buckingham, 9
Vire (Normandy), 2
Vossius, Gerardus/Gerrit
   Janszoon Vos, 145 n. 287

William I the Conqueror, king
   of England, 12
William II Rufus, king of
   England, 12–13
William the Aetheling, 13–14,
   72 n. 72
William of Saint-Thierry, 68 n.
   65, 97 n. 127

Index of Scriptural Citations

The numbering of the Psalms is that of the Vulgate.

Gen		*Luke*	
3:19	142 n. 274	1:77	110 n. 157
26:5	104 n. 146	2:29	122 n. 182
		6:29	91 n. 117
Job		12:43-44	108 n. 154
29:18	67 n. 62	17:3	148 n. 293
Ps		*John*	
6:6	104 n. 145	7:38	115 n. 166
50:12, 19	119 n. 176		
55:12	90 n. 113	*Acts*	
79:6	106 n. 153	9:16	106 n. 151
83:11	67 n. 64, 68 n. 65	18:3	142 n. 275
115:15	101 n. 138		
		Rom	
Lam		7:24	94 n. 123
3:19	129 n. 197	8:23	94 n. 123
3:28	67 n. 61		
3:30	129 n. 196	*1 Cor*	
		13:4-8	86 n. 105, 93 n. 119
Eccl			
1:2	89 n. 111	*2 Thess*	
12:8	89 n. 111	3:10	83 n. 99, 140 n. 262
		Phil	
Matt		2:3	145 n. 285
5:40	91 n. 117	2:7	97 n. 129
6:34	94 n. 121		
7:13-14	129 n. 198	*Heb*	
11:30	105 n. 148	11:17-19	104 n. 146
18:15	148 n. 293		
24:13	105 n. 149	*1 Pet*	
25:1-13	118 n. 172	2:7	102 n. 141
27:13-14	117 n. 170	5:8	133 n. 218, 150 n. 303

www.ingramcontent.com/pod-product-compliance
Lightning Source LLC
Chambersburg PA
CBHW030443300426
44112CB00009B/1132